The Church's hidden asset

The Church's hidden asset

Empowering the older generation

Michael Apichella

Kevin Mayhew

First published in 2001 by
KEVIN MAYHEW LTD
Buxhall
Stowmarket
Suffolk IP14 3BW

© 2001 Michael Apichella

ISBN 1 84003 701 6
Catalogue No. 1500413

9 8 7 6 5 4 3 2 1 0

Cover design by Jonathan Stroulger
Edited and typeset by Margaret Lambeth

Printed in Great Britain

CONTENTS

This book is lovingly dedicated to Sue Geiringer – sister, mentor, and friend.

Prologue

THE SEASONS OF LIFE

I

Winter. The jagged and hard season of death – crusted over with frost, outlined in galvanised, black edges. Life is stayed for a time. But the Old Ones know that it will not always be winter. Full of faith, like wise squirrels hoarding acorns in a dead oak tree, they rest in the knowledge of the life to come. But not all agree which of the remaining three seasons is the True One.

II

For some, it is the aftermath of the winter famine, spring. The first fragrant rain nourishes grey, stark woodlands. Mocking the faltering blasts of wind, ice thaws. Hope grows. Joy produces the nodding snowdrop and the green-shafted daffodil. An excited flutter of downy fledglings try their wings. Spring is evidence of things not seen but hoped for.

III

Others say it is kind-hearted summer: predictable and orderly, not capricious like spring. The breeze kisses the land softly on the mouth – spreading the sacred incense of roses, honeysuckle and mint. The Old Ones hold that summer is the time for maturing, for growth, for yielding the fruits of love: joy, peace, patience, kindness, goodness, faithfulness, gentleness and self-control.

IV

And so comes golden autumn. There is a damp scent of mould in the air. A chill settles on the ground like the dew. The ruby sun sinks lower and lower in the western sky with each passing day. It is a time of endings: green leaves, brown-edged and curled. It is the season of bonfires, burning and consuming in hot red and pale orange flames all that has not lived up to its calling. Glowing cherry embers and black ash. Billowing white smoke. *Can God be in this*? Perhaps. For now comes the harvest. Russet apples and plump pears; yellow corn and chalky wheat; fat carrots; the jolly pumpkin. In autumn all will enter into the storehouse. All? All who have allowed God to plant them like a seed; all who have yielded to God's plough, and tiller; spade and hoe. God's pruning knife. All whom he has harvested.

And here is the reality: winter is no season but death eternal; the three seasons are a Holy Trinity. One cannot exist without the others. Like the godhead, one season in three; eternal in fruitfulness, in wisdom, in compassion and in glory. One day all will live or die eternally. The Old Ones gradually realise it. They hold out this message to the Young Ones, a generation not eager to listen; a generation not expecting death for a long, long time; a generation eager to seize and bite and taste, and then to draw its own conclusion about the seasons of life.

Introduction

WHAT DOES IT FEEL LIKE TO BE OLD?

Everything takes longer to do.

I forget that I'm old. Is memory loss a sign of old age? (Laughter)

I've had a good innings. It's time to step aside and make room for younger people.

For many elderly people, having grey hair and wrinkles is tantamount to being surplus to requirement, especially when it comes to feeling useful. A while back, I gave a talk to a group of retired men and women. The talk was entitled 'God's Grey Warriors'. I told them that the *Concise Oxford English Dictionary* defines 'warrior' as 'a veteran soldier of any fighting service'. My point was although they may be pensioners in the world's eyes, they are 'active duty' warriors in God's eyes. These gentle, quiet people seemed amused that I thought of them as warriors. The fact is, the older we get, the more useful we become to God.

Consider Abraham and Sarah. They were nearly 100 before God saw fit to make them parents. Look at Moses' life. We might think that the first half of his life was wasted. But God used the passing decades to transform Moses from a fugitive into a lawgiver, from a follower into a leader of a nation. Simeon and Anna performed their greatest service to God in old age when they proclaimed Jesus as the Messiah (Luke 2:25-38). What if they had decided they were no longer needed in old age? Today, thousands of elderly men and women retire from serving God before he has finished with them. Someone or something seems to have convinced them that younger people are better suited to carry on the work of the Church. If you were Satan, which segment of your enemy would you want to fight, the seasoned veterans of many hard-fought campaigns or the fresh troops just out of training?

During the Vietnam War, the United States had a policy of making soldiers redundant after two years of combat. Just as the soldiers gained sufficient experience to confront the enemy effectively, they were pulled out and replaced with inexperienced troops. The result was defeat for the world's superpower. Might the Church be guilty of making its most experienced warriors redundant? Are we telling the elderly they are not needed? And if so, why are the elderly so underappreciated?

This book is a reminder to the Church that old people are a rich natural resource with a vital part to play today. Their lives should be brimming with opportunities to serve God. This is not to say the older generation is inherently better than the younger; that would be patent nonsense. Today's younger generation is full of idealism and virtue.

My hope is to encourage a genuine partnership between young and old. The lives of the saints testify to how well old and young work in concert. Think about Eli and Samuel, Ruth and Naomi, and Paul and Timothy. As long as the Church is divided its mission on earth is undermined. Truly, together is better. The last chapter of this book develops this concept more fully.

In the meantime, I hope to establish that God has work for us in every season of our lives, but especially in old age. To help focus our minds on this fact, each chapter concludes with an exercise. These are to heighten awareness of the role that only the elderly may play in the mission of the Church. Remember, God has no mandatory retirement age. As the psalmist writes: '[They are] planted in the house of God, they flourish in the courts of our God. *They still bring forth fruit in old age . . .* ' (Psalm 92:13-14)

Part One

THE AGE OF USEFULNESS

Chapter 1

THE BIBLE HONOURS THE ELDERLY

Overview: In the Bible we are reminded that the elders in our midst are to be esteemed.

A biblical view of old age

Try to imagine what our society would be like if we seriously adopted the Bible's attitude towards the elderly: 'My son, obey your father's commands and do not neglect your mother's teaching' (Proverbs 6:20). 'Likewise you that are younger be subject to the elders' (1 Peter 5:5). Such ideas are contrary to our youth-orientated way of thinking.

The Catholic social critic Robert Leckie has said no age in history has ever worshipped at the altar of youth as ours does.[1] Cinema critic Richard Corliss agrees. He exposes our culture's bias against the elderly in a commentary published in *Time* magazine: Many movies these days are 'spinning fables in which youth is its own reward' and old age is to be avoided.[2] Patricia Ireland, president of the National Organisation for Women (USA), warns that ageism is endemic in western culture: 'There is still that undercurrent of when you see grey, it means the fire has gone out.'[3]

Ageism is an odious social ill which may be defined as a deep and pro-found prejudice against the elderly. Sadly, ageism flourishes even within the Church. A curate once complained bitterly, 'I'm not sure what we're doing wrong at my church. Sunday after Sunday, our pews are filled with old people.' Indeed, many churches make it a policy that none of their Elders may be older than 50. Arguably, a church overflowing with youth promises a bright future and is often the hallmark of a successful ministry, but how might God view churches that actively discriminate against the old when he ordered that the congregations should honour the elders?

The term *elders* has many special meanings in the Bible. One of the most common applications refers to Jewish elders as an assembly of aged or at least well-experienced men, denoting seniority as in Luke 22:66, or in Acts 22:5, when Paul refers to the high priests as witnesses. In 1 Timothy 4:14,

Paul admonishes the youthful Timothy to be mindful of the gift he received after ministry from the elders.

In the early Church, then, elders performed crucial clerical and spiritual duties such as prophesying and laying on of hands. The younger generation held the elderly in high esteem regardless of rank or office. This is why we should shower the elderly with kindness and respect.

Campaign for real elders

Someone once tried to invent a microwave fireplace. When asked why anyone would want such a thing, he replied: 'So you can spend a whole evening in front of the fire in just eight minutes.' The problem is a microwave fireplace is nonsense. So is microwave maturity! It takes a lifetime to become who God wants us to be: 'And I am sure that he who began a good work in you will bring it to completion at the day of Jesus Christ' (Philippians 1:6). When it comes to serving God, old age is a distinct advantage. God wants masters, not apprentices, leading his Church. This is why we must make the most of the elderly, for by long experience they have become wise in the ways of the Lord. As the Psalmist suggests:

> The years of our life are threescore and ten, or even by reason of strength fourscore . . . So teach us to number our days that we may get a heart of wisdom. (Psalms 90:10, 12)

Undoubtedly, God uses youth in vital ways as we will consider in Chapter 11. It does not follow, however, that the old are inferior in comparison. Gifts and talents are spread liberally throughout congregations, and they are without respect to age. In teaching about special spiritual gifts, Paul points out, 'To each is given the manifestation of the Spirit for the common good' (1 Corinthians 12:7). This means that God equips every church with the necessary spiritual resources to sustain its life and spread its influence. Since the old are as vital as the young when it comes to using their special gifts and talents, ageism weakens the mission of the Church.

What are the gifts and talents unique to the elderly? It's hard to say. Certainly, with age comes a subtle wisdom that gives a different insight into life.

Sadly, a generation obsessed with staying young is not interested in knowing about the subtleties of old age. Pop icon Bob Dylan found this out the hard way. Dylan wrote the song 'Forever Young' when he was only 32 years old. It was for his son. The greatest blessing Dylan could think to offer his child at the time was that the boy might be spared the humiliation of growing old. It is significant that Dylan wrote this song, for he is credited with being the voice of the youth culture that grew up following World War Two. Perhaps best known is Dylan's 'The Times They Are A-Changin', which may be regarded as the first pop lyric warning parents that children would no longer respect and obey them. 'This is definitely a song with a purpose,' Dylan said. 'I knew exactly what I wanted to say and for whom I wanted to say it to [sic] . . .'[4]

The mature Dylan no longer writes ageist songs. According to Dylan, he much prefers to sing about how he sees the world today. Ironically, his current music puts him in conflict with the youth culture he helped to nurture. Many of his concerts in recent years have been disrupted by booing and slow-hand-clapping youths bent on forcing Dylan to sing his early songs. Dylan complained, 'College kids showed the most disrespect . . . I mean it was fierce. And all hell would break loose . . . [they would yell] "We want rock and roll" [and] lots of other things I don't even want to repeat, just really filthy mouth stuff.'[5] In 1998, Bob Dylan fell victim to his own invention. His popularity among the under-30 set was eclipsed by the Generation X group, Boyzone.

Now that Bob Dylan is in his 60s and his body and mind have slowed down, he writes songs reflecting wisdom that comes with grey hair. But youthful fans don't want wisdom, they want fun.

The elders in our midst today are among our greatest assets. Is the Church listening to them, or are they relegated to the lower divisions? The elders of ancient Israel played in the First Division. They were the grey beards upon whom Moses relied to make decisions, to direct the affairs of the people and to make announcements and policies of great importance.

According to historians Joan Comay and Ronald Brownrigg, the elders had a very important role to play. For instance, the elders announced the institution of the Passover, and they accompanied Moses up Mount Sinai to meet with God. On the settlement of Canaan, elders functioned in each town and were consulted by the central government. On the return from exile in Babylon, the elders continued to function locally, forming a third grade of laymen within the Sanhedrin or central council of justice.

Comay and Brownrigg state that the elders were very important in the New Testament era as well. For example, it was the elders of Capernaum who came to Jesus to ask him to help the Roman centurion: 'For he loves our nation, and he built us our synagogue.' (Luke 7:3-5)

In matters of biblical interpretation, too, the elders continued the ancient traditions handed down from father to son. This 'tradition of the elders' took the form of an endless extemporisation and extension of the Old Testament Law to enable its application in all circumstances. [6]

It must be conceded that under this system, the law became a great burden to bear for ordinary men and women. Jesus himself said of the custom, 'So, for the sake of your tradition, you have made void the word of God' (Matthew 15:1-9). Having said that, Jesus' criticism is an indictment of sinful human nature corrupting one of God's institutions, not an attack on the elders system. Not surprisingly, only a few years after the resurrection, elders or presbyters were greatly venerated officers appointed to look after key pastoral duties within the body of Christ: 'Let the elders who rule well be considered worthy of double honour, especially those who labour in preaching and teaching . . . Never admit any charge against an elder except on the evidence of two or three witnesses.' (1 Timothy 5:17-19) [7]

Comay and Brownrigg say that Paul prompted Titus to select elders in every town on the island of Crete. However, at least ten years before these letters were written, Paul had himself already appointed elders at Ephesus to whom on his last journey to Jerusalem he gave these final instructions:

> Take heed to yourselves and to all the flock, in which the Holy Spirit **has made you guardians**, to feed the Church of the Lord which he obtained with his own blood. I know that after my departure fierce wolves will come in among you, not sparing the flock; and from among your own selves will arise men speaking perverse things, to draw away the disciples after them. Therefore, be alert, remembering that for three years I did not cease day or night to admonish every one with tears. And now I commend you to God and to the word of his grace, which is able to build you up and to give you the inheritance among all those who are sanctified.
> (Acts 20:28-32, my emphasis)

Notice how Paul naturally expects the elders to guard the minds and souls of the younger members of the congregation, not the other way around. Why? Paul knew that when it comes to satanic deceptions, the older ones, having more life experience, are harder to fool than the younger ones.

As it is in heaven

Revelation shows that elders continue to enjoy their high calling even in heaven:

> And I heard a voice from heaven like the sound of many waters and like the sound of loud thunder; the voice I heard was like the sound

*of harpers playing on their harps, and they sang a new song before the throne and before the four living creatures and **before the elders**. (Revelation 14:2-3, my emphasis)* [8]

John is classified as a prophet, and his book is a prophecy. As such, his vision of the elders in heaven is accurate and trustworthy. Bible scholar George R. Berry points out in his Greek-English New Testament Lexicon that the elders John describes are in fact 'the heavenly Sanhedrin', [9] the same system of leadership by elders which existed in Jesus' day.

Honour the elderly

The fifth commandment admonishes: 'Honour your father and your mother, so that you may live long in the land the Lord your God is giving you' (Exodus 20:12). There is more in this command than merely the order to honour and respect our elders. Notice the second part of that command. It makes a promise that by honouring them, we will live long and prosper. Similar admonitions appear in Proverbs: 'Whoever curses his father or mother, his lamp will be put out in deep darkness' and 'Listen to you father, who gave you life, and do not despise your mother when she is old' (Proverbs 20:20; 23:22). Paul makes the same point: 'Children, obey your parents in the Lord, for this is right. Honour your father and your mother, which is the first commandment with promise: that it may be well with you and you may live long on the earth' (Ephesians 6:1-3); and, 'Do not rebuke an older man but exhort him as you would a father; treat older women like mothers' (1 Timothy 5:1-2). What is behind such instruction? God calls us to venerate parents in particular and the elderly in general because not only does he want us to appreciate their inherent value, but he also wants us to benefit from their long experience!

To consider

- When I was the Religious Programme Organiser at BBC Radio Oxford, each week I had to make important decisions that would affect the Sunday morning programme. One task I dreaded was selecting the music we would play. On my staff was Edith, a shy, retired midwife then in her 70s. Although she had had a responsible and active career, when I knew her, she was content to do behind-the-scenes clerical jobs, which are vitally important for a successful radio programme, yet not at all glamorous. I recall asking Edith for advice, one Sunday early in my career, on the choice of music for a broadcast. After I had shown her my selection, she looked dubious. 'I think you'll find,' she said kindly, 'that your choices really are not suitable for the season of the year. It's Passiontide.' She suggested some more sedate music that might be more suitable.

Annoyed that Edith didn't give me the confirmation I was actually seeking, I snorted, 'Who cares about the seasons of the Church year? These lyrics really explain the Gospel message.' Edith simply shrugged, and in the end I played the music I had selected. The letters from our listeners that week and the critical comments of a colleague – an ordained minister – proved to me that Edith had been right and I had been wrong. You may be sure that I paid closer attention to Edith after that *faux pas*.

- I go to a gym three days a week. There, I hear a great deal about wholeness when it comes to keeping our bodies fit. The trainer advises, 'Work the legs on Monday, the torso on Wednesday, and the arms on Friday.' We need to think holistically about exercising the gifting of the entire body of believers – the Church. Like muscles, gifts atrophy. Use them or lose them!

To do

Today I was in a tearing rush. Hurrying out of the house I jumped into my car, started the engine and pulled into the street as if each second I could shave off the thirty-minute drive to work would make a difference. As I approached the junction at the top of my road, I could see a maroon car. A grey-haired woman, diminutive and tweedy, sat behind the wheel.

'C'mon lady,' I said aloud as I eased in the clutch and pressed the brake. 'You're going to make me late!' I squeezed the wheel and gritted my teeth as she continued to hover at the intersection, tentatively looking this way and that.

From where I sat, I could see there was only one car coming, and that was a hundred yards away and moving slowly. Although I resisted the urge to sound my horn, I caught myself thinking, 'Old drivers are a menace and shouldn't be allowed on the road after the age of 65.' Then I recalled the book I was writing.

Have you ever caught yourself putting the elderly into unflattering pigeonholes? With some imagination and a sense of fun, the following experiment could drive home the point that very few people fit the neat, preconceived stereotypes we sometimes try to put them in – not least the elderly.

Ask members of your church to act out the following situations, showing how they think the elderly might act. Remember, the situations ought to be impromptu.

ACT I

- A senior citizen at the head of a long queue at the Post Office
- An old man and woman trying to programme a VCR
- An old person trying to log on to the Internet
- An old man or woman phoning in to a radio chat programme to comment on asylum seekers, body piercing, the state of the city's pavements, youth today, etc.

ACT II

After the group has had a bit of fun, turn the tables by asking them to act out the way in which their own grandparents, parents or other elderly relatives and friends might act in the same situations. Don't be surprised if the people suddenly act differently!

I recall doing this activity with some youngsters. One boy was having a great time sending up an old man in the Post Office. He was shaking and walking with a stick and forgetting where he had put his glasses. Nevertheless, when he was asked to do the same scene showing how his grandfather might act in the same scenario, he said indignantly, 'My Granddad plays football with me and my brother!'

This activity could lead to a general discussion about the changes made for Act II, shedding light on the way we all make unfair assumptions about the old.

According to Dr Francis Oakley, 'Research shows that there is generally no distinction between the performance of older and younger workers. Most studies find that older workers compare well with their younger counter-parts by measures of knowledge, output, reliability, and work habits.'[10] Oakley cites Peter Peterson's book *Gray Dawn: How the Coming Age Wave Will Transform America – and the World*. 'Where they do sometimes fall behind (for instance, in physical stamina), they make up for in judgement and experience,' he says. [11]

Once we stop viewing the elderly in an impersonal and uncaring manner and begin to view them realistically, then we may begin to appreciate just how important each old person is in God's eyes.

References

1   Robert Leckie, *These Are My Heroes*, New York: Random House, 1964.

2   Richard Corliss, 'The prince of prepuberty grows up', *Time*, 1 August 1988, p. 2.

3   Sara Terry, 'Older women's newer models', *Christian Science Monitor* (Boston), 9 June 2000.

4   Notes from 'Solid Rock' included in the 3-compact-disc Deluxe Edition of *Bob Dylan Biography*, C3K 38830, Columbia, 1985, CBS Inc.

5   Ibid.

6   Joan Comay and Ronald Brownrigg, *'Philistines' Who's Who in the Bible*, New York: Bonanza, 1980, p. 97.

7   Ibid.

8   Ibid.

9   George R. Berry, *The Amplified Bible*, note p.1492. Michigan: Zondervan Publishing House, 1987.

10   Dr Francis Oakley, TIAA-CREF Participant May 2000.

11   Ibid.

Chapter 2

THE OLD TESTAMENT PARADIGM

Overview: God's greatest Old Testament servants were elderly when they best served his purposes. This chapter focuses on the lives of Noah, Abraham and Sarah, Joseph and Daniel: five people who served God in their old age.

Noah

Of all the Patriarchs, Noah suffers from the worst public image. What do you think of when you think of Noah? Do you imagine an off-beat man more like Doctor Doolittle than a dignified commander-in-chief? Do you see him as an absent-minded but well-meaning crank that likes animals better than he likes people? If this is your image of Noah, you need to reconsider. Imagine John Stott, C. S. Lewis, Derek Prince and Pope John XXIII rolled into one, and you get one of the Bible's most important men, Noah.

Noah was respected everywhere in the ancient Near East. The Hebrews believed that Noah was the grandfather of all the races in this area, being venerated in many cultures and many religions for his faithfulness to God and his service to humankind and the animal kingdom. Noah lived in a corrupt and violent age very much worse than our own (Genesis 6:11). This fact led to God's terrible decision to destroy the human race with a flood.

Noah was very old when he built the ark (Genesis 7:6) and it is important to note that Noah foreshadowed the salvation by grace to be found in Christ. The New Testament writers confirm this.

The apostle Peter writes, 'For if God . . . did not spare the ancient world, but preserved Noah, a herald of righteousness, with seven other persons, when he brought a flood upon the world of the ungodly . . . then the Lord knows how to rescue the godly from trial.' (2 Peter 2:5, 9)

The writer of Hebrews also pays tribute to Noah: 'By faith, Noah, being warned by God concerning events as yet unseen, took heed and constructed an ark for the saving of his household; by this he condemned the world and became an heir of the righteousness which comes by faith' (Hebrews 11:7). Bible scholar and author Watchman Nee draws a correlation between Noah and all baptised believers alive today:

> Today when believers are baptised they go symbolically through water, just as Noah passed in the ark through the waters . . . And this passage through water signifies their escape from the world, their exodus from the system of things that, with its prince, is under the divine sentence . . . When you come up, you come up in Christ, in the ark that rides the waves, but your world stays behind. For you, that world is . . . drowned like Noah's, put to death in the death of Christ and never to be revived. [1]

Not long ago the daughter of a professor at a well-known Christian College was a guest in our home. A bright young woman with a vibrant faith in God, she was keen to join us at our Sunday service. Afterwards, I asked what she thought of the sermon and she replied, 'I was getting a lot out of it until the minister began to talk about Noah as if he actually existed.' She explained that her professors all say that Noah was a literary device invented by the Hebrew poets. I believe that Noah existed. What's more, I accept the account of a global flood. This may prompt you to roll your eyes, but I say it puts me in good company. I have already shown that the Apostle Peter and the writer of Hebrews believed in Noah and the flood. So did countless other saints and Bible scholars; and so did Jesus Christ, who used Noah and the flood as an object lesson to teach his disciples about the doctrine of the Second Coming:

> As were the days of Noah, so will be the coming of the Son of Man. For as in those days before the flood they were eating and drinking, marrying and giving in marriage, until the day when Noah entered the ark, and they did not know until the flood came and swept them all away, so will be the coming of the Son of Man.
> (Matthew 24:37-39)

If you are tempted to think that you are too old to be of any use to God, keep this in mind. Noah was well past retirement age when God said: 'I will establish my covenant with you' (Genesis 6:18). Remember, with God, all things are possible!

Abraham and Sarah

Now let's consider Abraham and Sarah. In the Jewish, Christian and Muslim traditions, the patriarch Abraham emerges as a father figure, dignified, firm in faith, humane, and respected by the local rulers wherever he went. He was a relatively young man when he left the booming metropolis of Ur and moved up river to Haran (Genesis 11:31). Later, at Haran, God actually appeared to him and said 'Go to the land that I will show you' (Genesis 12:1). Here the Lord promised to 'make a great nation' of him. When Abram, as he was then called, left Haran with his wife, he was 75, an age we might consider to be a hindrance in serving God. On the contrary, their age was not a hindrance to God's plans, it was a prerequisite!

No doubt Abram and Sarai tried to start a family in anticipation of the fulfilment of God's promise that they were to be parents to an entire nation. Gradually, however, it became apparent that Sarai and Abram were unable to conceive. In order to help fulfil God's promise, Sarai ordered Hagar, her younger maid, to have sexual intercourse with Abram. The folly of this course of action was proved when Sarai found herself torn by animosity towards her maid and the baby, Ishmael, who had been fathered by Abram (Genesis 16). Although the decision for Abram to have a child by his wife's maid was perfectly legal according to the culture of the day, Abram's and Sarai's mistake was to assume that God was somehow in error when he said an old woman could become pregnant.

Put another way, Sarai may have felt frustrated and useless due to her apparent infertility and old age. The feeling of futility is a common complaint of the elderly today, and there is no reason why an old woman living two thousand years before the birth of Christ would not have felt the same when circumstances became too much for her to bear. Even people of deep faith may become embittered, so it is easy to empathise with Sarai's resentment when she actually blamed God for her childless state, 'Behold now, the Lord has *prevented* me from having children . . . And Abram hearkened to the voice of Sarai.' (Genesis 16:2, my italics)

When Abram was 100, he was sure that he and Sarai were to be a childless couple. Again God spoke to him, promising to make a great nation of him. God clearly stated that his wife, now called Sarah, would be 'a mother of nations, and kings of peoples would come from her.' Hearing this, Abram, now called Abraham, 'fell on his face and laughed, and said to himself, "Shall a child be born to a man who is 100 years old? Shall Sarah, who is 90 years old, bear a child?"'(Genesis 17:15-17). Shortly after, while three heavenly visitors were being entertained in Abraham's tent, the Lord again foretold that Sarah would have a son. As the words were spoken, 'Sarah was listening at the tent door behind him. Now Abraham and Sarah were old, advanced in age; it had ceased to be with Sarah after the manner of women. So Sarah laughed to herself, saying, 'After I have grown old, and my husband is old, shall I have pleasure?' (Genesis 18:10-12)

It's worthwhile to note that in recording their doubt, the Bible spares no punches when it comes to portraying these people as they really were. Here we see old age, not in an idealised form, but as it really is.

While many excellent books have been written about Abraham dealing with his faithfulness in the face of impossible circumstances, my point is this: it's important that we are willing to do God's will despite the limitations imposed upon us by advanced years. For it is this very willingness that enables human beings to open themselves up to the overwhelming compulsion of the Holy Spirit, without whom nothing could ever be done to advance the cause of God.

Thanks to the mysterious work of the Holy Spirit in us, the more aged, weak or infirm we are, the greater the works God is able to do through us – provided we are willing. As Paul writes to the Church at Corinth: 'For the sake of Christ, then, I am content with weaknesses . . . for when I am weak, then I am strong.' (2 Corinthians 12:10)

Abraham and Sarah understood this same principle Paul writes about: despite their scepticism and the biological fact that an elderly couple could not be fertile, they faithfully acted upon God's promise. The result? An old man and an old woman believed and became parents, thereby giving rise to the Jewish nation that would ultimately produce the royal lineage of Jesus Christ and give rise to the Church as we know it today.

Joseph

Let's examine Joseph. In his youth, Joseph was a spoiled boy who gloated over the fact that his father Jacob favoured him above his ten older bothers, as indicated by the coat of many colours Jacob had presented to Joseph. Actually, evangelist J. John points out that the translation for the gift is better rendered as 'long-sleeved coat', but that's not such a catchy title for a West-End musical!

One day Joseph told his brothers about a dream he had had that indicated that he was destined to rule over them. This was unheard of in that culture, for the eldest was the heir and the one to assume leadership over the clan after the father had died. Following this insult, Joseph's siblings began to plot ways of getting rid of their braggart little bother.

The story of how Joseph's kin betrayed him is told in Genesis 37-40.

Although his brothers' treachery was meant for evil, God used this event to start Joseph's gradual rise to power under Potiphar, captain of Pharaoh's guard.

Another man might have been angry at the way in which his brothers had abused him, and might have used his gradually acquired powers to have his revenge, but Joseph decided that he would honour God by forgiving his siblings. Because of this, Joseph was instrumental in preserving the covenant between God and Abraham by welcoming his father Jacob and his brothers into the land of Goshen during a famine in their home land of Canaan. (Genesis 42-47)

It is incorrect to think that Joseph's special mission ended after he had seen his family safely settled in Egypt. In fact, Joseph's work was to continue for many more years, during which time he continued to rule wisely and show kindness to his brothers: 'So Joseph dwelt in Egypt, he and his father's house; and Joseph lived a hundred-and-ten years.' (Genesis 50:22)

At this ripe old age, Joseph was prompted by the Holy Spirit to utter one of his greatest prophesies over the nation of Israel, which at that time was little more than a scattering of refugees: 'I am about to die; but God will visit you, and bring you up out of this land to the land which he swore to Abraham, to Isaac, and to Jacob.' (Genesis 50:24)

Daniel

Many people picture Daniel as a youthful, idealistic man. Certainly, he was young when he interpreted King Nebuchadnezzar's dreams (Daniel 2). He was also relatively young when he became governor of the province of Babylon. But Daniel's life didn't end there; in many ways this time in his life was merely the prelude. When King Belshazzar saw the ghostly handwriting on the wall in about 539 BC, Daniel was in his 60s and well-known for his godly wisdom. Naturally, he was asked to interpret the cryptic message. It was then that the mature prophet preached his most powerful sermon, ending with the fatal prediction for Belshazzar: 'Your kingdom is finished . . . you are weighed and found wanting . . . your kingdom is divided and given to the Medes and Persians.'

Under the rule of the Medes and Persians, it was this prophet's steadfast faith in God, born of years of faithful living, which prompted King Darius to order all his subjects to honour the God of Israel.

To consider

In Psalm 71:18, the poet writes, 'So even to old age and grey hairs, O God, do not forsake me, till I proclaim thy might to all generations to come.' I was reminded of the significance of this statement a few years ago when I had the honour of meeting Queen Elizabeth, the Queen Mother, at a garden party. I was invited to meet her by virtue of my association with the Fulbright Foundation in Washington DC and, as I mingled with the other guests at London's Commonwealth Institute on the big day, I was caught up in the spirit of the event.

When at last it was announced that our royal hostess had arrived, I was very disappointed to find myself at the rump of a very long receiving line. I craned my neck and stood on tiptoe trying to steal a glimpse of the great lady. After an hour of fruitless anticipation, I fell on to a plate of succulent cucumber sandwiches and made small talk with a guy from Buffalo, New York.

'It looks as if we won't get to meet the old gal,' I said.

'You can say that again,' he groused.

I stuffed another cucumber sandwich into my mouth just as a guard approached us and said, 'Prepare to meet the Queen Mother.' My eyes bulged and the hors-d'oeuvre stuck to the roof of my mouth. Suddenly, the man from Buffalo and I were standing face to face with the Queen Mother. 'How do you do?' she said to my companion who was frantically loading his camera with a roll of film.

While he was speaking to the Queen Mother, I stole a glance at my first flesh-and-blood queen. Her gown was an exquisite shade somewhere between emerald and violet. She wore a matching hat the size of a small cathedral, which on anyone else would look ridiculous. On her it was – well, regal. To my amazement the Queen Mother turned to me and said, 'Thank you for coming today. And how are you finding your stay in Britain?'

'Great!' I replied grinning broadly, praying nothing was stuck in my teeth. Still holding my hand, the Queen Mother made more polite talk and then moved on to greet some other guests.

Everyone to whom I later spoke commented on how the Queen Mum had made each one feel welcome despite the many guests waiting to meet her. I was amazed at her high level of energy and patience. But what struck me most of all was the Queen Mum's smile – it was like the smile of someone I'd known since childhood.

At 100, the Queen Mother continues to be a national treasure, and generates millions of pounds for the treasury by attracting tourists from all corners of the world. But to measure her worth in crass commercial terms is to do the great lady a grave injustice. Behind her magnetism lies a deep Christian faith.

A few years ago, the Queen Mother had heard that one of her staff had become a Christian. The next day, she presented him with a Bible and some of C. S. Lewis' works. The man said that the books were a big help to him in understanding his newly found Christian faith.

During the celebration at St Paul's Cathedral marking the Queen Mother's one-hundredth birthday, the Archbishop of Canterbury, Dr George Carey, ended his remarks by saying that the gifts of age – wisdom, humour, tolerance, patience and courage – are often disregarded in our culture. 'But these are gifts we are proud to honour here today.'

He continued, 'At a time when such a premium is placed on the young and the new, it is glorious indeed to be celebrating the birthday of someone who can help us travel that country called "life". And someone, indeed, who so fully continues to inhabit it.'

In closing, he added an impromptu 'Thank you and God bless you, our dear Queen Mother.'[2]

To do

Arguably, as with fine wine, old age brings about certain improvements.

Can we learn anything from the lives of Noah, Joseph, Daniel and the Queen Mother? I think so. Old age is brimming with potential for fruitful ministry.

1. How may the gifts and talents of the oldest members of your community be utilised?

2. When you are looking for people to serve in your church or group, remember the following advice:

   a. Avoid dismissing old people. They have lived longer and have greater experience in life.

   b. Every person, no matter what age, needs the opportunity to give as well as receive.

   c. Christian growth continues until death.

d. 'Every-member' ministry means just that. It is unfair and short-sighted to think that the old have no worth. Retired people are more often in touch with the natural rhythm of time. Allow them to help others resist the pressures of the rat race.

e. God is, in fact, the oldest person alive. Think about it. He does.

A special note for discussion among members of urban churches: *Asian and African immigrants in the spotlight*

In Asia and Africa the old enjoy a privileged place in society. Whether in the home or in the community, the elderly contribute significantly to the welfare of their families; in return, they are looked after and venerated by the younger family members, especially when they become sick and feeble. Sadly, the closely-knit family is disintegrating among Asians in the United Kingdom. According to Ben Gamadia, one of Age Concern's project organisers, '. . . as the young Asians adapt to the Western way of life, they are no longer content to live with their parents and the traditional extended family is breaking up.'[3]

John Carvel, social affairs editor of the *Guardian* writes:

> *Elderly people from the Pakistani and Bangladeshi communities in Britain are far more likely to suffer from multiple deprivation than their Indian or white contemporaries, according to a survey of the over-60s published . . . by the Office for National Statistics.*
>
> *It found 28 per cent of older Pakistanis and Bangladeshis were in households with no central heating that were more likely to suffer from dampness and condensation. And 38 per cent lived in over-crowded homes with more than one person per room.*
>
> *They were almost three times as likely to live in a household without a phone than white, Indian or black Caribbean older people.*
>
> *The report said the ethnic dimension of social inequality among older people could no longer be overlooked. There were nearly 250,000 over-60s from ethnic minority groups, and this number was set to swell as these groups aged.*[4]

In the 1980s, Age Concern pioneered projects for elderly Asians in those mainly urban areas where they are the majority. One very successful scheme is the Luncheon Club popular with Asians because they are fond of gathering to eat as a social activity. The Social Services Department now recruit more Asian home helps. 'Meals on Wheels' offer a variety of vegetarian selections for Hindu clients.

Is your church or organisation willing to modify existing schemes in order to reach out to all the elderly in its area, overlooking ethnic, racial or religious barriers? Like Age Concern, the Social Services and 'Meals on Wheels', are we willing to respect the customs and the needs of people who are different from us? If yes, how?

If we hope to bring the good news of the Gospel to all of our neighbours, we must be prepared to start building bridges wherever possible. Let's dare to reach out in love to all who need us, including the elderly non-Christians who are also our neighbours. As St Francis of Assisi said, 'Preach the Gospel by every means possible. Use words if necessary.'

References

1   Excerpt from Watchman Nee, *Classics from Watchman Nee*, vol 2, Kingsway Books.

2   Robert Hardman, 'God bless you, Queen Mother', *Daily Telegraph*, 12 July, 2000, p. 1.

3   Andrea Waind, 'When age is no longer golden', *Sunday Times*, 26 June 1988, p. C4.

4   John Carvel, 'Deprivation study pinpoints ethnic divide among elderly', *Guardian Unlimited* Online: Wednesday, 13 September 2000.

Chapter 3

THE NEW TESTAMENT PARADIGM

Overview: God's greatest New Testament servants were also elderly when they best served his purposes. This chapter focuses on the lives of Peter and Paul, Simeon and Anna, and the poor widow – five people who honoured God in their old age. Secular history also proves the worth of the elderly.

Peter and Paul

'You aren't getting older; you're getting better.' This is, of course, a cliché and one with a distinctly patronising ring. Nevertheless, it is true.

In the New Testament, Paul and Peter's performance ratings certainly improved with old age and experience. The young Paul was headstrong and vitriolic, quarrelling with Barnabus and refusing to forgive John Mark's youthful indiscretion:

> And after some days Paul said to Barnabas, 'Come, let us return and visit the brethren in every city where we proclaimed the word of the Lord, and see how they are.' And Barnabas wanted to take with them John called Mark.

> But Paul thought best not to take with them one who had withdrawn from them in Pamphylia, and had not gone with them to the work. And there arose a sharp contention, so that they separated from each other; Barnabas took Mark with him and sailed away to Cyprus, but Paul chose Silas and departed . . . (Acts 15:36-40)

The older, wiser Paul spoke the language of diplomacy. Incidentally, Paul refers to himself as an ambassador – also translated as 'old man' – in Philemon 9.

Young Peter was subject to emotional outbursts which in at least one incident led to Jesus' having to tell Peter in front of the other apostles that he would soon prove to be a coward (Matthew 26:31-35). Another low point for Peter, caused by the combination of his relative youth and inexperience as well as his tendency to act on feelings, not faith, was the time Jesus foretold his death and resurrection and Second Coming. Peter scolded Jesus for such ludicrous talk! The result? Jesus accused Peter of treachery:

> From that time Jesus began to show his disciples that he must go to Jerusalem and suffer many things from the elders and chief priests and scribes, and be killed, and on the third day be raised. And Peter took him and began to rebuke him, saying, 'God forbid, Lord! This shall never happen to you.' But he turned and said to Peter, 'Get behind me Satan! You are a hindrance to me; for you are not on the side of God, but of men.' (Matthew 16:21-23)

On the other hand, with the accumulation of grey hair, Peter gained much wisdom. Young Peter tried and failed to walk on water (Matthew 14:28-30); old Peter healed Aeneas, the paralytic at Lydda, and he raised Dorcas to life (Acts 9:32-42). In old age, he alone among the believers in Jerusalem could hear God speak when men half his age heard only the rumblings of their own prejudices.

Consequently, the elderly Bishop Peter, relying on his experiences and his long years of walking obediently in the Master's footsteps, persuaded James and the other leaders to allow Paul to preach the Gospel to the Gentiles. James announced, 'Brethren, listen to me. Simeon (Peter) has related how God first visited the Gentiles, to take out of them a people for his name. And with this the words of the prophets agree . . .' (Acts 15:6-15). This pronouncement gave rise to the birth of the Church.

Simeon and Anna

Along with wisdom comes an increase in patience as we age. Certainly Simeon and Anna faithfully played their role in God's Kingdom, waiting until they were both well into their 80s before God acted in their lives.

God selected Simeon and Anna to proclaim the Messiah (Luke 2:25-38). Tellingly, one might think that after Simeon had proclaimed the baby Jesus as the long-awaited Messiah, his service was done. Now he could die a happy old man who had reached the zenith of his years by making his startling revelation. But no. God had yet another task for Simeon to perform. Simeon was to speak another word prophetic from God over Jesus.

As Simeon gave back the child Jesus into his mother's arms, he blessed Mary and Joseph, and then he uttered an enigmatic prophesy: 'Behold, this child is set for the fall and rising of many in Israel, and for a sign that is spoken against (and a sword will pierce through your own soul also), that thoughts out of many hearts may be revealed' (Luke 2:34-35). These words have been taken to refer to the grief suffered by his mother Mary at his crucifixion.

A final word about Simeon as pointed out by Church historian Ronald Brownrigg: As a younger man, he had been shown that he would not die without seeing 'the Lord's Christ'. Taking the baby Jesus in his feeble arms, Simeon powerfully blessed God, saying the words of the Nunc Dimittis, the prayer that has become a pillar of the Christian Church:

> Lord, now lettest thou thy servant depart in peace, according to thy word;
> for mine eyes have seen thy salvation which thou hast prepared
> in the presence of all peoples, a light for revelation to the Gentiles,
> and for glory to thy people Israel. (Luke 2:29-32)

The poor widow

In Mark 12:38-40, we read that Jesus had been teaching about the unscrupulous scribes who, among other violations of the law, were wont to 'devour widows' houses'. Jesus always treated widows with sympathy and respect, and so it is all the more telling that Mark records that at precisely the next moment, Jesus sat opposite the Temple treasury and watched the faithful putting money into the collection receptacles.

Typically, many wealthy people put in large sums – the equivalent of thousands of pounds. But when a poor widow slipped two coppers into the coffer, Jesus stopped what he was doing and pointed out the old woman. 'And he called his disciples to him, and said to them, "Truly, I say to you, this poor widow has put in more than all those who are contributing to the treasury. For they all contributed out of their abundance; but she out of her poverty has put in everything she had, her whole living."' (Mark 12: 43-44)

Because this story is so well known, it has become something of a cliché. That is a great shame, for few in our welfare state may fully comprehend what it meant for the old widow literally to give away all she had.

What motivated the woman? Clearly, it was an act of trust meant to glorify God, but where does one find the faith to act in this way? I believe that her faith grew over many years of trusting God to meet her needs – physical, mental, and emotional. What's more, I believe that her faith was the result of a deep conviction that the Lord would not allow her charity to cause her to starve. To give away all that one has for God's sake is the act of a person who has had a long and nourishing relationship with God, a relationship that had been growing over many years.

Examples from secular history

Secular history is full of people who have played a vital role in the world well into their old age. The world is far richer for the contributions of Casals, Monet, Barbara McClintock, and Albert Schweitzer.

Pablo Casals (1876-1973) was a Spanish cellist, conductor, composer, pianist and humanitarian who was a leading musician of the twentieth century. To try to rid the world of war, Casals composed the oratorio *El Pesebre* (The Manger), 1960, which he conducted throughout the world. His reminiscences are contained in *Conversations with Casals*, recorded in 1955 by Josep Maria Corredor. His reflections on his life were published as *Joys and Sorrows* (1970). In 1989 the National Academy of Recording Arts and Sciences recognized Casals with a posthumous Grammy Lifetime Achievement Award.

Claude Monet (1840-1926) was one of the French impressionist painters who brought the study of light to the attention of the art world. Known as the Father of Impressionism, he was in his 50s when he began his famous series of water lilies. From around 1916 to 1921, when he was 81 years old, he worked on a series of the same subject that forms a continuous band of paintings completely surrounding the viewer. These paintings were donated by the artist to the state and eventually, in 1921, installed in the Musée de l'Orangerie in the Tuileries Gardens, Paris. Despite failing eyesight, Monet continued to paint almost up to the time of his death, on 5 December 1926, at Giverny.

Barbara McClintock (1902-92) was an American geneticist and Nobel laureate most noted for her discovery that genes can transfer their positions on chromosomes; this is important for the understanding of hereditary processes. She obtained her doctorate in botany from Cornell University (USA) in 1927 and became affiliated with the Carnegie Institution of Washington in 1941. She was awarded the Nobel Prize for physiology and medicine at the age of 81 for her life-long achievement.

Albert Schweitzer (1875-1965) was a German theologian, philosopher, musicologist, medical missionary, and Nobel laureate. Schweitzer built an important hospital and equipped it to provide care for thousands of Africans, including 300 lepers. Throughout his long life, he returned frequently to Europe to lecture and give organ recitals; in 1949 he visited the United States. He received the 1952 Nobel Peace Prize when he was 77. His important work continued right up to his death on 4 September 1965, in his ninetieth year.

Michelangelo was 71 years old when he was appointed chief architect of St Peter's in Rome. From then until his death at 89 he worked on his masterpieces, including the fresco 'The Last Judgement' which so astounded Pope Paul III that when he first saw it on Christmas Day in 1541, he could only drop on his knees and gaze up in awe at Michelangelo's work. Interestingly, as the artist aged, his insights into spiritual matters reflected 'new light'. Even as popes and kings heaped praise on his work, Michelangelo came to see his accomplishments as mere dung in contrast to the works of the true Master.

According to art historian Diane Kelder,

> [Michelangelo] confessed . . . a great fatigue with painting. More and more, he sought solace in religion; the sonnets he wrote in the 1550s expressed disillusionment with the part painting and sculpture had played in his life:
>
> Now know I well how that fond phantasy
> which made my soul the worshipper and the thrall
> of earthly art is vain; how criminal
> is that which all men seek unwillingly . . .
> Painting nor sculpture now can lull to rest
> my soul, that returns to his great love on high,
> whose arms to clasp us on the cross were spread.[1]

Are these the words of an old fool? They seem more like the words of a wise man who has lived long and reached a threshold where he is able to look into two worlds – time and eternity – and to judge wisely the true meaning of life and his own place within it.

The achievements of Casals, Monet, McClintock, Schweitzer and Michelangelo prove that people may carry on making significant contributions to their communities, their friends and their families well into old age. Indeed, often age improves the quality of service. As with silver, gold, Persian rugs or fine wine, age enhances value in the eye of the discerning beholder. The expanding population aged 65 and over is one of our most important, and most neglected, natural resources. In the United Kingdom, there are 10.6 million people over 65:

- 8,940,000 in England
- 917,000 in Scotland

- 583,000 in Wales
- 253,000 in Northern Ireland. [2]

It is easy to see the above numbers just as statistics. But these aren't mere numbers on a sheet: they represent grandfathers and grandmothers, uncles and aunts, neighbours and friends. The collective common sense and insight of these older saints are frequently ignored and lie like buried treasure just waiting to be discovered by society. But because our society largely discounts the wisdom of the elderly, their gifts remain buried treasure, ignored by a generation teeming with knowledge, but sadly lacking in wisdom.

To consider

In the last decade, many people have begun to rediscover the wisdom of their elders (what I refer to here as traditional values). For a growing number of women, their grandmother's values are suddenly in style again. That's the message of *A Return to Modesty* by author Wendy Shalit. With dexterity and passion Shalit dares to admit that the values of her grandmother's generation – modesty, chastity and fidelity, values so much scorned today – offer the only formula for lasting happiness and fulfilment.

To do

- Read *A Return to Modesty* by Wendy Shalit, and Danielle Crittenden's *What Our Mothers Didn't Tell Us: Why Happiness Eludes the Modern Woman*. See if you agree with their findings.

- It is an enlightening exercise to investigate how our contemporary values are at odds with those of the previous generations. Take time and make notes when you are reading classic novels or watching old films. Pay attention to how people interact with one another. See how communities functioned. Note the roles the elderly play. When you have put your research down on paper, discuss your findings. What conclusions may be drawn from this exercise?

- Try to become more aware of the words you use to describe old people. Make a list of adjectives and nouns that refer to old people, places or things. Don't do this in one sitting. If you are a leader or a parent, you may unwittingly be passing on limiting prejudices and unhelpful attitudes to younger people.

As we have seen in the previous chapters, the majority of God's greatest servants were what we might call Senior Citizens when they reached their stride in their walk of faith with God. Paul and Peter, Simeon and Anna, and the widow commended by Jesus – these people should inspire us. We see, too, from secular history that without the elderly our culture would be poorer in art, science, sociology and architecture.

Significantly, today we are witnessing a backlash against the culture of youth with its emphasis on instant gratification. People today do not want pat answers nor do they want theories. They want to know what works, and for a growing number of people, young and old, a return to the values of the Bible may contain just the answers they are seeking.

The churches have many occasions in which to take the lead. We must create opportunities for the older members of our congregations to work in tandem with younger people. Then the whole congregation may be involved in the mission of the Church, which began with Abraham and Sarah, continues to this day, and shall continue until Christ returns.

References

1   Kelder, Diane, *Pageant of the Renaissance*, Praeger: Pall Mall, 1969.

2   Age Concern statistic, 2000.

Chapter 4

CONTRIBUTIONS MADE BY THE ELDERLY

Overview: In this chapter we examine the role the elderly play in effecting great changes in the lives of people around them.

Wisdom born of experience

If God told you he would grant you one wish, what would you ask for? Good health? Personal happiness? Wealth? King Solomon was the son and successor of King David. In a dream, God asked Solomon what he would like to possess most of all. The king said: 'That I may discern between good and evil' (1 Kings 3:9). The Lord was so pleased that Solomon did not ask for personal wealth, he promised him this as well. Thereafter, Solomon became renowned for his great understanding.[1]

The Bible says that Solomon's wisdom was unsurpassed (1 Kings 4:30, 31). It is also said that he composed over 4000 proverbs and songs; moreover, he was learned in zoology and botany.[2] Solomon knew that God expects men and women to serve him into old age:

> O God, from my youth thou has taught me,
> and I still proclaim they wondrous deeds.
> So even to old age and grey hairs,
> O God, do not forsake me,
> till I proclaim thy might
> to all the generations to come.
> (Psalm 71:17-18)

In this chapter, I want to focus on the lives of some lesser-known people who faithfully served God 'even to old age and grey hairs.' In Chapter 1, I mentioned how, as a BBC producer, I ignored the musical advice of my older, wiser assistant, Edith. That incident is only one mundane example of how a younger person may benefit from the wisdom of an elder. A far more serious example may be found in 2 Chronicles in the Old Testament.

King Rehoboam

Following the death of King Solomon, Rehoboam his son ruled in his place. When Jeroboam the son of Nebat heard that Solomon was dead, he pressed the new king, saying, 'Your father made our yoke heavy. Now therefore lighten the hard service of your father and his heavy yoke upon us, and we will serve you.' (2 Chronicles 10:4)

To his credit, King Rehoboam consulted with the old men of the court who had advised Solomon, asking them for their advice. They replied, 'If you will be kind to this people and please them, and speak good words to them, then they will be your servants for ever.' Immediately, the king sought out his friends, the young men with whom he had grown up, and he asked them for their advice. They were unanimous in advising Rehoboam to remain firm and unyielding to Jeroboam's request for leniency.

Rehoboam ignored the advice of the senior advisors and the result was catastrophic for the nation of Israel. When it became clear that the new king intended to add to the miseries of his people, a revolt erupted among the ten tribes which led to the splitting in two of Israel – the Kingdom of the North (Israel) and the Kingdom of the South (Judah). In the midst of this revolt, 'King Rehoboam made haste to mount his chariot, to flee to Jerusalem. So Israel has been in rebellion against the house of David to this day' (10:18-19). Rehoboam should have listened to the advice of his elders in this instance. It would have changed the course of history.

Now let's examine the lives of some contemporary saints whose years of experience have taught them to change the course of history for the better.

Bloom where you are transplanted

Born in County Durham in 1910, Mildred Bell Serjeant was well known in Suffolk for her prophetic ministry and her indefatigable championing of women's causes. Sadly, Sister Serjeant died before this book was published. But if there is one thing I have learned from her long life, it's that it requires many years of life to see all of God's promises fulfilled.

Sister Serjeant contracted polio when she was a child, resulting in one leg being shorter than the other. During an evangelistic meeting in 1927, she limped forward for healing. After the minister laid hands on her and prayed, her leg was miraculously lengthened. Later her doctor confirmed that the polio had been healed. In 1931, Sister Serjeant entered Bible College where she was ordained as an Assembly of God minister in 1934.

During this time, she was privileged to work under Smith Wigglesworth. It was then she received a prophecy promising she would be the mother of a multitude of boys from foreign lands: 'Thou shalt see them. They shall come, from the north, the south, the east and the west; male children shall be born unto you. You shall nurse them, nourish them, and teach them to go.'

Sister Serjeant admits the promise from God was very puzzling. She really had no idea how this would happen. 'But,' said Sister Serjeant, 'as Smith Wigglesworth used to say – only believe! So I did.'

In 1933, Sister Serjeant was sent to pioneer a church on the edge of the Fens in sleepy West Suffolk. 'I didn't want to go there,' confided Sister Serjeant. 'It was so rural, so unlike what I was used to. But I felt that doing God's will was more important than doing my own. So I packed my bags and went.'

Not much happened for the next ten years. However, after the Second World War broke out in Europe, West Suffolk suddenly became a hive of activity. Air bases sprang up around Suffolk like mushrooms. Literally overnight, Lakenheath and nearby Mildenhall became home to hundreds of British, colonial and American airmen. By 1944, boys from Pennsylvania, Ohio, California, Texas, Nevada, Montana, Alaska, Hawaii, New Zealand, Australia, Canada, Scotland, Ireland, Wales and England moved into the tiny village of Lakenheath. Many came with a strong Pentecostal faith and so sought out fellowship in Sister Serjeant's Assembly of God Church. Others had no faith of any kind, yet they fell under the power of the Holy Spirit when they heard this godly woman preach the Gospel at open-air meetings or in the church.

Boys of all sizes and nationalities converged on Sister Serjeant's home. They came for food, advice, prayer and Bible studies. Many became regulars; other boys came just once, only to die in the bombing raids over enemy territory. Truly, Sister Serjeant 'nursed them, nourished them, and taught them to go.' In the fifty years after the war, Sister Serjeant continued to minister to those that came to her for help.

Moreover, old age did not bring an end to her own spiritual growth. As each decade passed, she became bolder in her faith. With hindsight, she admitted that in the early years she was somewhat timid. Over the years, though, she began to see that by being hesitant she had failed God. 'Brother Wigglesworth used to say to me, "You know you can't treat the devil lightly. You have to be rough with him. You have to mean business." That taught me a great lesson, and ever since, I have sought to use the authority that the Lord has given us in the name which is the name to which every knee will one day bow, and every one will confess that Jesus

Christ is Lord. Thank God we have a name that is above every other name, and God has given us authority in that name – Jesus Christ!'

Prior to her death, Sister Serjeant slowed considerably. Yet she remained a spiritual mother to the forces stationed at RAF Lakenheath and RAF Mildenhall. My own family received wonderful hospitality from her in 1997 when we were trying to buy a house in Suffolk. When Sister Serjeant heard that a family with young children had no place to stay, she gave up the entire top floor of her home and fed all seven of us.

What had Sister Serjeant learned through her many decades of serving God? Without a moment's hesitation she declared, 'Doing God's will is better than attaining worldly success.'

I turned in my 9-mm pistol for an NIV Bible

Billy McFetridge was a vicious killer in the late 1970s. An angry young man, he had attained the rank of captain in the UDA, a paramilitary organisation that flourished in the Belfast area at that time. Today, Billy is a Christian evangelist with an international outreach to ex-prisoners and street people.

But how did Billy come to meet Jesus as his personal Lord and Saviour; and more to the point, what has his story to do with a book extolling the virtues of old age? Billy tells his story:

I was arrested on 17 September 1980. After days of intensive grilling by the police, I finally confessed to my crimes, including one I did not commit – the murder of a man I'll call John Smith. This false confession was to come back to haunt me in less than a year. Meantime, I was put in the Crumlin Road Prison in Belfast on remand. It was there I got to know two older Christians who were to change the course of my life: Bill Vance and Agnes Hancock.

A few months after I had been in the prison, I learned that Christianity is not merely a religion, it's a powerful way of life – and it existed inside prisons as well as outside. One day a prison officer came by and invited me to come to a Bible Study. I saw this as an ideal chance to get out of my cell for an extra hour or so a week, and so I said I would like to come along. I went to a small Bible Study led by the late Bill Vance, a very godly older man who had served in the prisons in Northern Ireland most of his life. Over the years, he led countless offenders to salvation in the Lord Jesus Christ.

Bill made an effort to get to know us prisoners. I could tell he had our interests at heart, and that he respected us despite our being behind bars. Because of this, prisoners were naturally drawn to Bill. What's more, Bill talked about the Bible as if everything was true. To him, the scriptures were as real as the morning's headlines. This was no milquetoast; this was a man's man. Through him, I came to learn that Jesus was real too – and not in merely the historic sense of real. Jesus was around today, and every bit as interested in the affairs of men in modern Ulster as he was in ancient Palestine. To say this was a radical revelation would be an understatement.

After a few months, I found that I was able to open up to Bill. Although I wasn't used to talking about my innermost emotions, fears and concerns, I found Bill was easy to talk to. He listened and seemed to understand me. We talked about prayer, and before long, my prayers stopped being cries into the darkness. Bill showed me that God was there listening to me when I spoke to him. Moreover, God replied to anyone who called to him. For the first time ever, my prayers became two-way conversations with God. Of course, I never heard God's voice with my ears, but I couldn't deny that he spoke to me in my mind, through certain situations and even other people – and not just prison chaplains.

Bill Vance was an important part of the next step in my walk of faith. Bill said that no man could change by himself. Only God could change us – the Bible calls it being born again (John 3:3). Quietly and alone one night in March 1981, I knelt in my cell in the Crumlin Road Prison, and invited Jesus into my heart to become my Saviour and Lord. I laid aside my weapons and my hate and placed my life and future under God's control as it says in 1 Peter 3:15: '. . . have reverence for Christ in your hearts and honour him as Lord.' By doing this, I began my life all over. 'When anyone is joined to Christ, he is a new being; the old is gone, the new has come' (2 Corinthians 5:17). There were no bells, nor were there any rockets when I had done it. It was much better than that. A quiet feeling of peace crested over my whole being like a gentle wave of the sea. For the first time ever, I felt one with God and with the universe – despite my being locked up in a cell miles from loved ones and the comforts of home.

It wasn't until September of 1981 that I was charged officially with my crimes. It was then, nearly a year after I had made my initial confession, that my having admitted to Smith's murder came back to plague me with a vengeance. Until then, I had not thought about this serious error I'd made. Now I was completely dumbfounded and terrified to hear from my lawyer that the police were planning to use this charge to put me away for good. 'Why on earth did I ever confess to a crime I hadn't committed?' I wailed as I paced around my tiny cell. Facing the prospect of this last charge, I knew that this one crime would be the test of whether or not I trusted that God had my best interest at heart. Despite my anguish, I slipped down on my knees and prayed simply, 'I commit this whole mess into your hands, Father. Thy will be done. Amen.'

Soon after, a second elderly person, the late Agnes Hancock, a prison visitor, entered my life just when I most needed her. One day she and another woman paid a call to my cell. I confided my situation to Agnes, who then shared my needs with some of her prayer partners outside of the prison.

Agnes turned out to be a beautiful Christian woman with a remarkable story of her own. She was very good to me while I was behind bars, and I found that at times when I was really struggling to find faith, Agnes would turn up or she would send a letter to me. This small kindness may not seem much to you; but to a man in prison awaiting a certain life-sentence, such contact is a lifeline.

One day I was agonising over my having signed that wretched confession. Sure as clock work, Agnes came to me, and as gently as my own mother she said, 'If you are innocent of this particular charge, then God will not allow you to be punished for it.' What struck me about the old woman's words was that they were spoken more like a prophecy than as mere words of condolence. As the trial began, the authorities were adamant that the murder charge stick. They had a signed confession. It would take nothing short of a miracle now to save me from being wrongly charged with a crime I'd not committed.

My defence fought well on my behalf in the courtroom, but privately my legal advisors were preparing me for the worst. One solicitor had said to me, 'The police have their piece of paper with your signature on it. That means this is an open and shut case. You never should have signed that confession, Billy. Don't be surprised if you go down for life.' My heart sunk at his words.

During the morning of the third week of my trial, I was feeling especially downcast, despite Agnes' words and the support of a network of prayer across Ulster on my behalf. My heart sunk even more when I met with my barrister in a downstairs room before the day's proceedings began. His face seemed to be hiding something as he sat down across from me. I feared the worst. 'Billy, I have some important news for you.' I waited to hear his words, fully expecting him to tell me he and his colleagues had thrown in the towel. 'I had a telephone call this morning from the

Department of Public Prosecution, and they informed me that in relation to your particular case, they would be prepared to drop the murder charge.'

I was shocked. I was too stunned to speak. 'Well, Billy? Are you relieved? It's just possible you won't be going to prison for life.'

'Of course, I'm relieved. This is great news,' I said. But my barrister put up his hand. 'There's one caveat, Billy. The deal is that they will drop the murder charge provided you'll plead guilty to manslaughter.'

'They've got a deal,' I retorted. I didn't have to think twice about it. My feet hardly touched the steps as I ascended the stairs to the courtroom. My guilty plea was accepted and at the end of my trial, I was charged with 58 offences under the Prevention of Terrorism Act. The total number of years to which I was sentenced came to 152 years. However, due to my plea-bargaining, I was to serve only 12 years imprisonment on the manslaughter charge. The remaining counts would be concurrent.

I thanked God that Agnes had come into my life when I needed the wisdom and faith of an older, wiser person to bolster my own fledgling faith. I hate to think how my life might have turned out had Bill and Agnes not taken a hand in guiding my life towards Christ.

Reg Simms

Not everyone is called to dramatic work, as were Bill Vance and Agnes Hancock. Many retired people may use their spare time to serve others in practical ways – shopping, fetching medical prescriptions, cooking meals, providing transport, visiting the sick, or caring for young children.

All Saints' Parish Church, Sidmouth, has a predominantly elderly congregation. The average age of house group leaders is between 55 and 76. Reg Simms, 76, described a popular church activity called 'Snack and Chat'. 'When someone is all alone, the opportunity to meet regularly for a snack and lively conversation means a great deal,' he said. 'We keep it informal. Everyone gets to know each other and lasting friendships are made.'

Reg believes that when people make themselves available to God for his use, age is no barrier. He became a churchwarden after retiring from the Electricity Board. Once his term ended, his vicar invited him to organise a house group. Recently he and his wife, Daphne, hosted an Alpha group. 'Our church has many opportunities for people our age to serve,' said Reg. 'All you have to do is ask.'

From Russia with love

Reg Simms is fighting fit. But what about the many unfortunate people who find their health ebbing in their later years? It takes a special kind of grace to say, 'Here I am, God; use me – just as I am.' People who are not afraid to speak to God this way find there is no end of important tasks needing their attention. Billy Graham tells a story about a remarkable old woman who lived in Moscow when Graham's books were contraband. Soviet churches were desperate to receive Christian books from the West that were very had to come by. Once one or two had got past the officials, the only way the material could be distributed was by making typed copies in the Russian language and handing them around to cell groups. The KGB was quick to figure out where illegal printing operations were housed, and so such operations were routinely closed down and the leaders put in jail.

One day an elderly woman volunteered to head an operation from her tiny flat. 'I will type up Dr Graham's books,' she offered. The leaders eyed her: she was literally bent double with arthritis and bound to a wheelchair. Her mottled hands were twisted, and her digits looked more like a bird's talons than fingers. 'But how can you type the books, Mother?' one of them asked kindly. The old woman extended her first finger and wiggled it. 'I can use this,' she said, grinning.

Reluctantly, they agreed to move the operation to her tower block. Slowly but surely, one manuscript after another was produced by her labour of love – pecking away with one good finger. As the books began to make the rounds of Moscow, the KGB went into a frenzy to discover who was running the illegal press. More than once, her building was thoroughly searched, but since the police knew she was a poor old widow crippled with arthritis, they never bothered to search her flat. And so the books continued to be typed out. Graham admits that when he heard of this woman, he was deeply humbled.

We must expose the lie that the old are of no use to others or God. King David was correct when he said of the elderly: they are 'planted in the house of the Lord, they flourish in the courts of our God. They are still bringing forth fruits in old age.' (Psalm 92:13-14)

The greying of Britain

The number of people over pensionable age is projected to increase. Allowing for the change in women's retirement age to 65:

- The population of pensionable age will rise from the current 10.7 million to 12 million by 2021.[3]

- These numbers will certainly be compounded because people in the West are living longer.

The rapid greying of Britain presents an unprecedented social phenomenon. On one hand, it will create grave medical, ethical and social problems that cannot be ignored. On the other, it will create wonderful opportunities for the elderly to contribute to their communities.

To consider

Octogenarian Billy Graham has observed, 'God has no retirement scheme for his children.' This means that through all the changing scenes of life, in sickness or in health, God expects us to put ourselves forward for him to use in any way he sees fit. Retired couple Michael and Judy Peters understand this. Here is their story.

Put your pension where your heart is.
Most businessmen and women nearing retirement dream of a second childhood in the sun. Not so for Michael and Judy Peters. Michael decided to put his pension where his heart is.

After retiring from Merston Peters Ltd of Bury St Edmunds, Suffolk, in 1999, Michael and his wife, Judy, decided to make themselves available to God for his service. 'Now that I'm retired, I want to do more with my faith,' said Michael. 'We decided to set up a Christian charitable trust which we've named Acts 1:8 which is taken from the New Testament Book of Acts, chapter One, verse Eight.'

'We hope to put something back into the community. I've been active in the Bury St Edmunds chapter of the Full Gospel Businessmen's Fellowship International; I'm also a field representative for the region and in that role co-ordinate the FGBMFI Seedtime Conference, a five-day event dedicated to supporting the work of the churches in and around Bury St Edmunds. But Judy and I feel that overseeing a charitable trust will open even greater possibilities for us to serve others.'

Michael remains the non-executive chairman of Merston Peters. In return, he has agreed to sell his shares back to the company with one proviso: that Merston Peters Ltd support the work of the trust. 'The objects of the charity are to co-ordinate teaching conferences, concerts, meetings and seminars in order to help churches in our area. We also plan to distribute Christian literature, videos and CDs. As part of my retirement package, Merston

Peters' managing director and I have agreed that 7.5 per cent of the company's profits will go to supporting Acts 1:8 for the next twenty-one years. This, plus the tax refund, will bring the figure up to around 10 per cent. We hope that as time goes on, the amount for distribution will be considerable.'

This bold venture may not seem a sensible thing to do with one's pension. However, for Michael and Judy, this isn't about sense, it's about faith. Judy added, 'The idea for a charity came about when Michael was appointed a trustee of an educational trust connected with a previous employer. The experience he gained prompted him to develop a strategy for his own charity.

'Actually, as a company we've supported many charities, and gradually the directors have grown to welcome the idea of giving relatively large sums of money away to worthy causes. We believe in tithing, both as a family and as a company; by that I mean being good stewards of our money, and giving back to God around 10 per cent of our income.'

'Although this income will be instrumental in ensuring the success of the charity, it is hoped that more will come from gifts,' said Michael. 'We are open to receiving contributions from individuals.'

Critics may point out that the charity may place too much emphasis on raising money. Michael is not worried though. 'We need not be afraid of criticism because we are not lining our pockets. We need money to carry out our principle objectives. We have set this charity up so that Judy and I and our trustees could have some say over how Merston Peters make their future charitable donations.

'The Christian trust is the vehicle for our ministry. There is always a need for teaching and evangelism and by putting some of our retirement money into a charitable trust we will ensure that the money and the focus of the work remain true to the original vision.'

The Peters know that they are taking a risk. But like the aged widow, who put her life's savings into the collection box in the Temple (Mark 12:43-44), the Peters have learned that it is better to put their money where their hearts are than to selfishly live for themselves. So what is the next step for Michael and Judy? 'It's up to God, now,' said Judy.

To do

The elderly can offer their lives up to God for his service regardless of the extent of their gifts and talents, or, more to the point, in spite of the limitations of old age or hard circumstances.

Our ability to be useful to God is limited to our attitude toward serving others. Make a list of practical things you can do to serve God in retirement. Here are a few suggestions for discussion and prayer:

- Use your home as a place to hold a Bible study or house group meeting

- Health and energy permitting, open your homes to others in need.

- Offer sympathy over a cup of tea

- Help young parents look after their children

- Provide a peaceful haven for an overworked or troubled person

- Use your skills to help young families set up and live within a budget

- Volunteer to be a prison visitor like Bill Vance and Agnes Hancock

- Invest your pension in Christian organisations such as Acts 1:8, or others that you may know of. God blesses a cheerful giver!

- Volunteer your services to mission agencies, many of whom are looking for short-term missionaries. Many retired professionals and skilled labourers go into developing countries where their skills make the difference between life and death for thousands of people.

Remember that God will bless your effort no matter how large or small.

Useful addresses

Acts 1:8
Mead House
Drinkstone Green
Bury St Edmunds
Suffolk IP30 9TL

References

1   Joan Comay and Ronald Brownrigg, *Philistines' Who's Who in the Bible*, New York: Bonanza Books, 1980, p. 360.

2   Ibid.

3   http://www.ace.org.uk/   (Age Concern Home Web Page)

Chapter 5

THE CHURCH'S WASTED RESOURCE

Overview: In this chapter we examine the role the elderly may play in the mission of the Church and community. In recent months, the elderly have realised they are a potent voting bloc which politicians will have to court or else suffer the consequences.

The flower fades

Bertie and Ben, both aged 80, were having coffee in Ben's kitchen. They were talking about growing old. Bertie complained, 'You know, I can't hear clearly any more!' Ben tut-tutted, saying, 'I don't have that problem, knock on wood!' As he rapped his knuckles on the table, he turned around, saying, 'Is that someone at my door?'

Ageing is a fact of life. The Bible compares our lives to that of a flower, implying that our time here on earth is for a fixed season and nothing may significantly prolong the allotted amount of time we have on earth.

The more we learn about the chemistry of living things, the more the Bible's metaphor takes on scientific relevance. Each of us begins life as a single microscopic cell. Through the process of mitosis, the cell begins to divide into more and more cells until there are billions of cells. Throughout our lives, cells are dying but are immediately replaced by new ones. But some cells, such as brain and heart cells are not replaced. When these particular cells die, they are lost for ever.

Ecclesiastes 3:1 states: 'For everything there is a season . . . a time to be born, and a time to die . . .' The microbiologist Leonard Hayflick has shown that the old preacher of Ecclesiastes was right. We all have a biological 'clock' which governs the lifespan of all organisms. By taking a type of skin cell from a very young human being, Hayflick found that at first the cells in the culture dishes grew and divided regularly, just as they would in the body. But then after about fifty divisions, the cells slowed their rate of multiplication, stopped dividing, and died. As he repeated this experiment, he used the skin of older people. The results were the same except that the older the skin cells, the fewer the times the cells divided. Later he used the cells of a liver. They, too, ceased to divide after a certain number of times. Hayflick calculated that about fifty divisions is just the number of times a living skin or liver cell would tend to divide in the human body in the lifetime of 100 to 115 years. So the individual cells of the body seem to be set to the same biological clock that governs the lifespan of the whole organism.[1]

Ageing is not shameful. Yet in our ageist culture it has become so. In an essay published by the British Baptist Union, Donald Black wrote, 'Perhaps we are fashioned more than we care to admit by the society of which we are part, which defines and then values people in terms of what they do, or what they have, rather than who they are.'[2] Black points out that our culture is shaped by two social systems – the reproductive and the productive system. The first deals with biological factors of reproduction and the raising of the young. The second is based on how adults organise themselves to produce goods and services in order to cause society to function. In the latter system, a premium is placed on an individual's ability to produce. According to Black, the elderly are especially at a disadvantage. This is because they are often functionally irrelevant, and they are often viewed as a burden instead of an asset to the rest of society.

A growing number of elderly people can't seem to cope with being surplus to requirement. Older men in particular are now at a greater risk of killing themselves than male adolescents and six times more likely to commit suicide than women of the same age. New mortality statistics reveal that the number of suicides among men over 85 in England and Wales rose by 40 per cent in 1999: Dr Michael Dennis, a psychiatry specialist at the University of Leicester said, 'Men are (most) affected by the loss of a significant role in later life. They are suffering from the work ethos of thinking they were once carrying out valued activities for society. With that comes hopelessness and despair.'[3]

The season of use

It breaks my heart to think of men in their 80s choosing to kill themselves because they feel worthless. Old age needn't be a time of despondency. Remember, God does not pension off his children once they reach the age of 65. In his book *Learning To Grow Old*, Paul Tournier quotes an elderly French poet who concedes that old age brings few pleasures, fading hopes for the accomplishments of life, and a wintry prospect on all that surrounds us. Yet the poet adds a third social system to those Donald Black describes. He says the third system is the season of use not toil.

Old age can be confusing and disillusioning if people don't know how best to use their time. Although they need toil no longer, whole new avenues of interest and service can open up if they have the eyes to see them. Old age should not be a time of barrenness and decline. Rather it should be a time when we concoct projects, ideas, schemes and adventures born of years of experience. We become idle and non-productive only when we think that we can no longer contribute to the family, the community, and the world.

Of course, we may have to do a little seeking to find some useful activity, but when we seek, we surely will find. My father-in-law was a top manager in the Electricity Board. When he took early retirement, my wife and I worried that he would become bored quickly because of the sudden change from the daily responsibility of making important decisions to the tranquil life of tending a small garden at home. We thought that boredom might lead to regret for having stepped down from his executive post a few years early. But, in fact, the years since he retired have been quietly fruitful. Almost immediately he began to step-up his involvement in his church. A few years ago, he and his wife hosted an Alpha Group in their home. Despite living on a fixed income, they support more charitable causes now than they did when they were on a salary. (I should know, for more than once, I have been on the receiving end of their largess!)

Older people find that they have more time to pray after they retire. In 1984 after leaving full-time teaching, I retrained to become a journalist. When my course was over, I began applying for jobs. But half a year later, I still hadn't found one! On an oppressively hot day, I was turned down for yet another job. I was miserable so, on my way home, I stopped at an ice-cream shop to cool off and cheer myself up.

As I licked my dripping chocolate cone, I overheard the shank of a conversation between a bald-headed old man and a very worried-looking boy of about 19. The old man whispered, 'I'll put it on the prayer list. Don't worry.' With that, the man produced a wad of dog-eared index cards and a stubby yellow pencil and scribbled something down. The boy left looking relieved.

I lost no time in introducing myself to the man, hoping he might offer to pray about my non-existent media career. 'The name's Bob,' he said. 'Sit down and tell me what's on your mind.' Now that I was nearer to him, I noticed his grubby Carnaby-Street jacket and rumpled white flares. His knees were frayed and he was missing a few teeth. I wondered if I'd made a mistake by thinking this odd man could help me. Still, I had nothing to lose, so I told him my story. When I had finished, I said, 'I heard you tell that boy that you would . . .' I felt my face flush bright red. 'That I'd pray for him?' he offered.

Tongue-tied, I nodded. 'Oh, I pray for a lot of people,' he assured me. Despite his absurd appearance, he turned out to be quite sane.

Bob had been a missionary for most of his life. After his health suddenly declined, he reluctantly returned home only to find convalescing not to his taste. He had a small pension and no commitments, so when he was well enough, he told God he still wanted to be used for Kingdom work. Gradually, Bob began meeting people around town and getting to know them.

'Nearly every one I meet has a need,' he told me. 'So I offer to pray for them.' He pointed to his index cards, a bundle as thick as a club sandwich. 'I make notes of people's needs, and then I go back to my room and spend the rest of the day on my knees praying through these,' he said, tapping a blunt forefinger on the cards. 'When you offer your services to God, he never refuses. Never.'

Bob put my name on his prayer list and tucked the stack away in an inside pocket. I'd love to say that I immediately found a job, but I didn't. In fact, my big break didn't materialise for another two years.

When I consider the incredible odds set against my getting a senior job with the BBC in a market such as Oxford, I am convinced that my break was the result of the prayers of a poor but faithful old man, proving again that God does not discriminate on the grounds of age, health or wealth.

At your service

No one can say categorically what older people are capable of doing. One thing is sure, if a person thinks he can do something but there is no opportunity to do it, then what that person thinks is of no importance. Therefore, it falls to church and community leaders to create genuine opportunities for the elderly to make contributions. Then the elderly will be able to use their considerable gifts and talents for the good of many, as well as for their own good. The reason why my father-in-law is so active in his church is due in part to his vicar, a younger man who sees the value in having older, more experienced men and women helping in the life of the parish.

In so many churches, the burden of administration, teaching, and any number of other non-pastoral duties falls upon the shoulders of the ministers. Moses faced this very problem in his own calling, and so he delegated elders to oversee many of the jobs that, though necessary, would pull him away from his main task. It doesn't take much vision to see how, for instance, someone who has retired from a job in banking might be called upon to oversee the church's finances and treasury. A mechanic might be called upon to keep the church's vehicles in good running order. A teacher might help to run the Christian education programme. A retired doctor or nurse might set up a scheme to educate others on wellness and general fitness. Those with no professional qualification are equally valuable. They may take the initiative in organising and hosting coffee mornings, church suppers, jumble sales, crèches or any number of social activities such as friendship clubs.

Much has been written lately of something called 'Friendship Evangelism'. Elderly church members may plan a meal and invite non-church members, friends and acquaintances to come along for something good to eat; this is followed by a lively talk given by another member of the church with an interesting story to tell. Near Christian holidays such as Easter, Christmas and Pentecost, the topics could be geared towards explaining some aspect of their faith.

In many communities where a shrinking tax base has meant that the local authorities have had to cut back on social services, churches may use their own funds and members to offer alternative services. After all, the modern social state is the offspring of an earlier Christian era marked by a sense of compassion. Non-Christians needn't worry that this is just a ploy used to make converts. There needn't be any mention of the name Jesus; a sincere desire to reach out and love others will do wonders for all concerned.

Like sharpens like

It is a well-known fact that people aged 65 and over represent a large percentage of people who attend church. Less well known is the rapid rate that older people are losing their faith today. According to Ben Summerskill of the *Observer*, 'New research confirming the trend will shock Britain's crisis-hit churches, which until now have regarded the elderly as the enduring backbone of their dwindling congregations.'[4]

According to Summerskill, researchers tracked hundreds of pensioners for over 20 years. The proportion that felt that religion was important to them fell from almost three-quarters to less than half. Involvement in organised religion also slumped, the research showed, amid a catalogue of complaints about established churches. The findings, he says, contradict the assumption that people turn to religion more actively as they confront approaching death.

> 'It has been assumed that older people's faith remained constant, but that no longer appears to be the case,' said Professor Peter Coleman of Southampton University, who conducted the research. 'This appears to be part of a general questioning of authority in society.'

> 'As I get older, I've had a few health problems and I now think more about death,' said 68-year-old David Terry, a retired college principal from Worcester. 'It now seems intellectually preposterous to me to maintain that there's a personal God who can alter actions as a result of prayer. I can no longer see any reason at all to think there's life after death, even though death is getting closer.'

> Terry, who was brought up and was once active in the Church of England, added: 'I still respect other people's beliefs. However, I'm certain that Roman Catholic and C of E faiths are increasingly irrelevant to many people. It's not death, but dying that most people now fear.'[5]

Summerskill spoke to a representative of the Humanist Society who said: 'This confirms the increased interest that we have seen from older people for some years. The older people are, the more they think carefully about these things. People realise that they can live good and responsible lives without the need for religion or superstition.'[6]

Why do an increasing number of elderly people see faith in God as irrelevant? Steve Chalke is known to many as the apostle to Generation X – that is the generation of young people between ages 12 and 24. Steve knows that to reach these kids, you need other kids, and so he trains and employs young Christians as evangelists. He knows that like sharpens like. So, the best way to reach the elderly is to commission men and women of faith from the same generation. Unfortunately, when it comes to outreach, most people leave the job to the younger generation.

Recently, I spoke at a church service held at a local retirement home. The youngest resident was in her late 60s and the oldest in her 90s. Of the seventy or so men and women there, only about twenty are committed Christians. As I preached, I felt compelled to end the service by inviting those present to pray with me that God would anoint them with the gift of evangelism so that they may reach the others in their community with the good news of the Gospel. I ended by suggesting they to turn to the person next to them and lay on hands to commission them to go out in the strength of the Holy Spirit. I'll never forget how excited some of them looked at the thought that at their age they were being commissioned to be evangelists in that home.

In every case I have mentioned, the participants may enjoy a win-win situation: the retired people find dignity and purpose, and the lonely or needy are welcomed into a non-threatening social atmosphere filled with like-minded, friendly people, and the mission of the Church is extended to an un-churched segment of society.

The emerging power of the grey vote

Considering that the fastest growing segment of our population is aged 50-plus, there is great potential for a grey revolution – not of bullets but of ballots. The first signs of revolution were noticed by political commentators in the summer of 2000 when the Government was accused by a coalition of Opposition members, age advocacy groups and unions for what has come to be seen as an unacceptably low rise in pensions. Prime Minister Tony Blair was warned that a 75p rise would be an insult to pensioners. According to Jack Jones, the president of the National Pensioners' Convention and former leader of the Transport and General Workers' Union, this meagre rise would not even buy a loaf of bread.

Shortly after this rise was announced, the now famous petrol revolt of September 2000 led some Government ministers to warn the Prime Minister of the consequences of an alliance between angry motorists and pensioners. Ministers warned Mr Blair that if the pensioners joined motorists, it would mean disaster for the Government. The press warned that pensions, not petrol should be Labour's priority as a third of the electorate is aged 55 or over, and they are more active in the voting process than younger segments of the population.

Mr Blair announced he 'got the message'; however, he would not change his policy, and he asked for the party loyal to support him on this issue. At the end of the 2000 Labour Party Conference, Tony Blair had been dealt a defeat when the Unions supported the 11 million pensioners, not the Government.

It is clear that the elderly, not junior members of society, will carry the most political clout in the future.

To consider

In Chapter 10 we will explore ways in which the Church may use both the young and the old working in conjunction to fulfil the mission of the Church – a mission which John Stott has said is a synthesis of evangelism, salvation, conversion with discipleship, and social welfare – as a means of preparing for the future work of the Church. Since churches already have a majority of older people in their congregations, we are in a good position to unleash experienced, wise, confident men and women who, like Abraham, Sarah, Moses, and countless other saints, have continued to serve God well into their 70s, 80s, 90s and beyond. But is the Church really ready for this?

We have heard so much about the pitiful waste of commodities hoarded by the European Community – the mountains of foodstuffs collected and waiting for use, but which will probably never be used. If the Church fails to cultivate the gifts and talents of its older members, we will be guilty of hoarding our own mountains of human potential, which under the right sort of direction, may be salt and light to a decaying and dark world. We cannot afford to allow the elderly to be the Church's wasted resource.

To do

Try making a skills inventory of your willing elderly members. You'll probably be in for quite a surprise at the talents going to waste. You may want to involve keen younger members of your congregation to conduct the inventories. This activity may be done in the older person's home, or somewhere mutually convenient. The following criteria could be a suitable basis:

- Full name and nicknames. (Be sure to ask how they received the nick-name if applicable. This leads to some interesting memories and tales, which help break the ice.)

- Address and telephone number, and email (optional)

- Have they got a car or access to other transport?

- List their hobbies, interests and leisure-time pursuits

- Work experience (prior to retirement)

- Special interests, talents and skills which you feel, may be of use to other members of the congregation.

As you can see, these are not prying questions which may be too personal or even hurtful. They are designed to help your congregation to:

- Discover unused gifts, talents and interests of the older people in their midst

- View older people as real human beings with interests and lots of human potential

- Increase a sense of self-worth through usefulness. (Older people need to see they are not useless or a burden to others.)

- Encourage members of the congregation to reach out to one another and thereby establish new networks of friendship among the different generations, as well as to help meet one another's needs in a Christ-centred atmosphere.

This exercise could be a valuable step towards using an important resource within most churches. You may find that many of the elderly members' special abilities might be just what are needed to deal with unexpected problems or special situations.

Make it a point to ensure that all the elderly members of your congregation are properly registered to vote. Those who are registered may not know where to cast their ballot or may need transport. With so many crucial issues facing the welfare of the elderly, there has never been a more crucial time for all people, no matter what their age, to see to it that their voice is heard at the ballot-box. For more ideas on how you can get involved politically at local and national levels contact:

The Christian Institute
26 Jesmond Road
Newcastle upon Tyne
NE2 4PQ

Email: info@christian.org.uk/
Website: http://www.christian.org.uk/

References

1   Kurt Finsterbush, (ed.), 'Snapshot of a changing America', *Sociology 1987-88*, University of Maryland: College Park, 1987, p. 82.

2   Donald D. Black, *Seniors* (Baptist Union), pp. 4-5.

3   Ben Summerskill, 'Suicide tragedy of the real-life Meldrews', *Observer*, 6 August, *Guardian Unlimited* Online, 15 September 2000.

4   Ben Summerskill, 'Elderly lose faith in religion' *Observer*, 3 September 2000, *Guardian Unlimited* Online, 16 September 2000.

5   Ibid.

6   Ibid.

Part Two

Be Not Conformed to the World

Chapter 6

THE CURRENT YOUTH CULTURE

Overview: In this chapter we consider the characteristics of the current youth culture, and investigate how it was formed. We end by exploring ways to bridge the generation gap.

Old is bad; young is good

In the 1984 United States presidential race, Walter Mondale, a fresh, 50-something presidential hopeful tried to discredit his 73-year-old opponent, Ronald Reagan, by claiming Reagan was too old to hold office. The media continually played up the issue, but the president simply ignored it.

During a live, televised debate, Mr Mondale raised the so-called 'age question'. The cameras cut to the president who was at last forced to comment publicly. With a slight grin, President Reagan retorted, 'I refuse to respond and thereby exploit, for my own political gain, my opponent's relative youth and inexperience.' The president had turned the issue on its head. The audience exploded with laughter, and the American voters thereafter perceived Reagan's age and experience as an asset, not as a liability.

Solomon, arguably the wisest man in the Bible, is credited with writing many of the sayings of the Book of Proverbs. Significantly, in the Proverbs, Wisdom is personified as an elder. The entire book is a treasury of ethical regulations and aids for living a long, healthy and happy life. These sayings cover a range of topics including knowledge, morality, chastity, self-control, selecting companions, laziness and justice. The author explains to readers his reason for setting down the proverbs:

> . . . that prudence may be given to the simple,
> knowledge and discretion to the youth. (Proverbs 1:4)

We have already seen in the previous chapters that God wants elders to lead his people. Some may ask, 'Don't leaders need the vitality, which is the domain of younger people?' Yes. But when it comes to decision- making, it is not always a question of vitality but of wisdom that matters most. The *Concise Oxford Dictionary* defines wisdom as '(Possession of) experience and knowledge, together with the power of applying them critically or practically'. Youth may have energy, but elders have experience, and more often than not, such experience may lead to wisdom.

Scripture: tried and found wanting?

The source of Christian wisdom is the Bible, a collection of books Jews and Christians understand to be a direct revelation from God. The Bible has greatly affected our culture. For centuries, many Members of Parliament fasted and prayed before voting on new laws. As recently as the 1940s, this nation observed days of prayer in times of crisis. Today, many politicians and journalists ignore biblical morality. The ethos of Proverbs is no longer politically correct, and ours has become a post-Christian nation. Tony Lane of London Bible College states:

> *Until the last century Christianity was all but universally seen in Christendom as a 'given', as a revelation from God which must be accepted by faith . . . But (today) the very idea of a revelation has been radically questioned . . .* [1]

How to identify the post-Christian youth culture

There are many characteristics of a post-Christian society. One very obvious one is that our post-Christian culture glorifies youth and demonises ageing. This happened slowly and imperceptibly as a result of many influences.

A few years ago, I was hiking with Dave, an old school friend. On the trail, we met some boys half our age. They sported spiky, dyed hair, outsized trousers that hung halfway down their backsides, and tattoos and studs on various parts of their bodies. We grunted our greetings to each other and carried on in opposite directions. After a few minutes, I said to Dave, 'You know, if we had dressed like that when we were at school, our friends would have fallen down laughing at us.'

Dave stopped and looked me over. He jabbed his thumb back at the kids we just passed: 'They'd rather die than wear what we wear.'

'But why?' I asked.

'Don't you remember how hard we tried not to look like our parents?'

Dave was right, of course.

It is important to identify four basic ingredients that distinguish a post-Christian youth culture, keeping in mind that you don't have to be young to be part of youth culture. The four are:

1. Distinctive dress

2. A tendency towards despair, death and promiscuous sexual behaviour

3. A general disregard for the values of the older generation

4. The adulation of pop idols.

Eccentric clothing, including a penchant for exposing underwear and wearing revealing clothing; tattoos, pierced bodies; extreme hairstyles meant to identify individuals with peer groups: these are hallmarks of the youth culture. But as Dave pointed out, such things are mere fashion statements, unsafe for determining anything consequential about today's youth.

Attitudes, the way people think and act, are far more significant. Today's youth culture is driven by a deep sense of despair, something foreign to previous generations of youths. The Scout Association of Australia has prepared some disturbing statistics based on teen deaths there:

> . . . *Youth suicide is a major and an increasing problem within the Australian community. For young people aged 15-24, we have one of the highest suicide rates in the world. This means that more than 400 young people in Australia die each year from suicide. The suicide rate of young people, especially males, has increased during the past two decades even though the suicide rate in adults has remained relatively static. The current rate of suicide is estimated to be around 15 per 100,000 for youths between 15-24 years of age. After traffic accidents, suicide is the leading cause of death in this age group. Between 1960 and 1990, the suicide rate tripled from 3.5 to 11.2 per 100,000. The male to female ratio has increased from 3:1 to 6:1 over the same period of time. The estimated suicide rate is still an underestimation of the true rate as deaths by suicide may be reported as accidental deaths or attributed to other causes.*[2]

Despite decades of government-sponsored health warnings and sex education, current youth culture is sexually permissive. Teenage pregnancy has increased worldwide over the last twenty-five years 'as a result of the weakening of social control by the family and community', according to the United Nations Population Fund. Sarah Boseley, health correspondent of the *Guardian* states that Britain has the highest pregnancy rate in Western

Europe among 15- to 19-year-olds.[3] Moreover, 'by age 16, one in four women in care are pregnant'.[4]

A general disregard for the values of the older generation is typified by the iconoclastic behaviour demonstrated by some young people at the 1999 Remembrance Day service held at the Cenotaph in London. Mobs of youths interrupted a solemn service, defaced war memorials, and screamed abuse at the soldiers, family members and others gathered to honour the men and women who gave their lives in defence of their country.

The above factors – distinctive dress; an obsession with death and sex; and a general disregard for the values of the older generation – epitomise youth culture. I'll come to the role of pop icons shortly; but first, let's analyse what has caused today's youth culture.

Birth of a generation

Sociologist Alvin Toffler suggests that today's youth culture is a product of the 1940s. The term 'teenager' (ages 13 to 19) had not been coined until then. In fact, he states, the word was virtually unknown in Britain until after the Second World War.[5] One contributing factor that gave rise to the youth culture is the 'accelerated thrust' of change in the West since the Second World War:

> For as the pace of change in the external environment steps up, the inner differences between young and old necessarily become more marked. In fact, the pace of change is already so blinding that even a few years can make a great difference in the life experience of the individual. This is why some brothers and sisters, separated in age by a mere three or four years, subjectively feel themselves to be members of quite different 'generations'.[6]

In the centuries proceeding our own, this rate of change was constant but not rapid. In the aftermath of the Second World War, however, the rate of change increased because of rapid advances in technology. Toffler theorises that young people stopped looking to the older generation as role models, and to other young people instead. This helped to create a 'youth ghetto . . . each with its own peculiar tribal characteristics, its own fads, fashions, heroes and villains'.[7]

This last point brings us to the role of pop icons – the heroes of the youth ghetto. In my opinion, the tide of youth culture came in three waves and took approximately thirty years to evolve into what it is today.

Let's consider the first wave of youth culture, roughly spanning 1946 to 1956. Frank Sinatra (easily the first pop icon) made an effort to oppose the values of the older generation by appearing on stage as a swaggering young romantic with loosened tie and tousled hair. He upset adults when he stirred the girls and made them swoon. By the time of Elvis Presley (1955), Sinatra was passé. Rock-and-roll with its uniform of blue jeans, a tight T-shirt and a black leather jacket had replaced the crooner's coat and tie. Romance was replaced by lust: even the term rock-and-roll is slang for sexual intercourse.

The next wave spanned 1956-1966. Bob Dylan, the Rolling Stones, and the Beatles typified the pop music idols; in cinema the icons were rebels Marlon Brando and James Dean; in literature the icons were beat poet Allen Ginsberg and novelist Jack Kerouac. They may be credited with the first overt call for youth to openly reject the culture of their elders. They advocated resistance to authority and urged young people everywhere to protest againtst the hypocrisy of the ruling classes.

If it may be argued that America led the way to a youth-dominated civilisation, then Britain perfected it. John Osborne's play *Look Back in Anger* (1956) became a wake-up call for a generation of 'angry young men'. Tom Stoppard and others wrote plays which held up a mirror to society as they saw it. In their plays, language frequently reflected deep frustration with an adult world that seemed increasingly irrelevant.[8]

In his book *Empire to Welfare State – English History 1906-1967*, T. O. Lloyd of Toronto University argues that Britain's contribution to the youth culture in the 1960s – the Beatles, Carnaby Street, and the mini-skirt – 'set the fashions for the young and provided stars for popular entertainment'.[9] They were 'an ironic echo of her (Britain's) position of dominance in other fields at the beginning of the century'. Lloyd adds that young British people wanted to forget their empire past (the jewel in the crown of the older generation) and focus on 'new fashions'.[10]

American Journalist Roberto Rivera points out that the three-day pop festival at Woodstock in August 1969 defined the third wave (1966-1976). This may be viewed as a world-wide symbol of the end of the rule of the elders and the beginning of the rule of youth: 'America, and perhaps the world, changed on those three rainy days on Max Yasgur's farm. At the very least, it marked the definitive triumph of America's youth culture. From August 1969 onward, what would matter in America, was what young people, and not their elders, thought.'[11]

Optimism is replaced by pessimism

It was Beatle John Lennon who opened the way for the flood of pessimism that was to mark youth culture. At the end of a routine interview, Lennon suggested that more people had heard of the Beatles than of Jesus Christ. Sadly, his words have proven true. One anthropologist stated that the Golden Arch of the McDonald's fast-food chain is better known to modern people than the cross of Jesus.

Why should a loss of biblical faith lead to a sense of pessimism? Consider pre-Christian sarcophagi. These show that death was seen by most cultures as the supreme tragedy. One pre-Christian tomb in Rome laments the demise of a young patrician: 'He went from the rosy prime of his life to being food for worms.' With the dawning of the Christian era, however, tragedy changed to victory through Jesus Christ's death on the cross and subsequent resurrection to life. 'Absent from the body but present with the Lord' became a typical epitaph found across tombs from North Africa to the Outer Hebrides; from Armenia to Ireland and beyond. As the apostle Paul put it: 'Death is swallowed up in victory. O death, where is thy victory? O death, where is thy sting?' (1 Corinthians 15:55)

As the youth population shrinks, youth culture must increase

Here's a riddle: What increases as it decreases? Answer? Youth culture. Demographics expert Peter Schwartz states that currently people under the age of 25 years make up more than half – 52 per cent – of the world's population. But by 2010, the population aged 0-24 years will be less than half of the total population in each of the world's regions except Africa, where it will be over 60 per cent. [12] This trend indicates a lowering, not an increasing, of youth population. It does not follow, however, that the current youth culture will dissipate. On the contrary. The generation gap will grow as technology grows.

What may we expect from the younger generation in the years ahead? 'Exuberance, exploration, confusion, and rebellion against old structures. It will be exacerbated by a newfound sense of power which teenagers . . . feel.' Moreover, 'Teenagers are not necessarily altruistic by nature; rather they are energetic and idealistic . . . . (and research shows) that idealism (will be) translated not into political sensibility but into either intense ambition or cynicism . . .' [13]

Unless youth culture is reconverted to biblical Christianity, the gap between the elderly and the young will continue to grow, making God's desire for unity between the young and the old virtually unachievable (see Chapter 11).

To consider

In the Bible, wisdom begins with 'the fear of the Lord' (Proverbs 1:7). Fear is better translated as awe and respect, not a painful emotion based on some threat. Even before sociologists determined that tomorrow's teenagers 'could be armies of nihilism and desperation',[14] demonstrating 'a constant insatiable hunger for fresh material – new music, new images, new fashions . . .'[15], the writer of Proverbs advised the elders to instruct the younger generation with sound advice and clear guidance for living their lives.

Merely preaching to younger people will not work. Youngsters respond to adults who form relationships with them. Once a relationship is forged – and this doesn't come easily – then there follows a natural exchange of ideas. Philosopher Dr Francis Schaeffer knew how important it is to relate in this way to youngsters. That's why he and his wife Edith founded the l'Abri Fellowship in Huemoz, Switzerland and Hampshire, England and elsewhere. In the late 'fifties and early 'sixties, a lost generation of young people made their way from all around the world to l'Abri (French for 'the shelter') where they found food, acceptance, approval and, most importantly, encountered older people in a loving atmosphere who were willing to listen to the younger generation. The Schaeffers listened as much as they spoke. And they did not dilute the scriptures trying to make them relevant. They preached sound orthodoxy. Dr Schaeffer summed up the task as follows: 'The problem which confronts us as we approach (youth) is not how we are to change Christian teaching in order to make it more palatable, for to do that would mean throwing away any chance of giving any real answer to man in despair; rather, it is the problem of how to communicate the gospel so that it is understood.'[16]

To do

Anyone who knows the history of the western Church during the period 1946 to 1976 will know that many ministers tried to accommodate rather than engage youth culture. The result was miracles were downplayed, discipleship was eschewed, and doctrine became subject to relativistic interpretation. Far from making the Church more appealing to young people, rather, the Church's influence went into decline.

Jesus loves you and so do I

How may adults reach out to the younger generation without compromising the message of the Bible? Many Christians feel that youth outreach is best left to the professional youth worker. Youth workers are highly dedicated people who do an admirable job, but they can't reach everyone.

Bruce and Kate Harris live in Suffolk with their four children. For years they felt someone ought to do something for the bored teens in their town. Then one day, they decided they themselves would do something. Kate explained, 'Our local church had a group up and running. The vicar asked us if we'd like to take it over. Bruce and I and our children discussed the idea, and took it on.'

Despite each having a busy schedule and myriad responsibilities raising their own children, they open their home once a fortnight for an informal evening of food, fun, and games. For each session they invite an interesting speaker to address some topic from a Christian perspective. 'This puts Christianity into a real-world context for youngsters who otherwise would see church as a boring weekly ritual with little bearing on their lives,' says Kate. Some weeks Bruce and Kate arrange talks about careers, travel, hobbies, or more serious topics such as death or abortion. 'Sometimes we do a straightforward Bible study, which isn't always so straightforward,' she said with a laugh. From time to time they skip the meeting and take the entire group to go skating or to see a football match, which suits Bruce – and the kids love it as well!

Are you willing to step out of your comfort zone in order to enter into a relationship with young people? Today so many families are broken, leaving emotionally scarred children in need of love and acceptance. If yours is a neighbourhood with many single-parent families, why not invite the youngsters into your life as Bruce and Kate have done?

Sociologists have noted that there is a special kinship between the very young and the very old. Well-known US author and People's Court Judge, Joseph Wapner credits his grandparents as having the strongest influence on his life:

> My earliest recollections (of my grandparents) is they took me seriously and listened – and talked – to me as if I were an adult. That means a great deal to the self-esteem of a child. If I have grown up to be a man with a concern for other people, and as a judge I must be, much of it was learned from my grandparents. [17]

Since this is so, are there retired men and women in your congregation who could act as surrogate grandparents for needy boys and girls? The concept of surrogate grandparents has been in practice in the USA for thirty years. Single or working parents are able to meet and choose willing retired people from their neighbourhoods who agree to help look after the children when needs arise. In Chicago's Uptown neighbourhood, a lonely boy picked up the telephone when he got home from school to an empty flat. He knew what number to ring. It had been provided by a local group of concerned retired people. When a volunteer answered the phone, the boy sobbed, 'I'm home alone, and I'm scared!' The listening grandparent, who was at least 55 years old and often housebound by disabilities, had quick words of assurance. The results show that the bonding that takes place between the children and the 'grandparents' is mutually beneficial.

As the generation gap continues to grow, steps must be taken to bridge that gap. National organisations in the USA such as the Retired Senior Volunteer Program are working to bring the old and the young together, but the most original and successful programmes are the ones created at the local level – such as the ones that you may form in your own church. So start to hatch your own ideas to build bridges between the generations. If you don't, the mistrust between the generations will only increase.

References

1   Tony Lane, 'Christian thought in the modern World', *The Lion Book of Christian Thought*, Oxford: Lion, 1992, p. 182.

2   The Scout Association of Australia and Dr Paul Lee. Published by the authority of the National Executive Committee of The Scout Association of Australia. Copyright © The Scout Association of Australia. First published in Australia, February 1996.

3   Sarah Boseley, 'Pregnant teenagers "had access to pill"', *Guardian Unlimited* Online, Friday, 18 August 2000.

4   Kendra Inman, 'Pregnant silence', *Guardian Unlimited* Online, Wednesday, 2 August 2000.

5   Alvin Toffler, *Future Shock*, New York: Random House, 1970, p. 257.

6   Ibid. p. 259.

7   Ibid. p. 258.

8   'Drama and Dramatic Arts', Microsoft ® Encarta. Copyright © 1994 Microsoft Corporation. Copyright © 1994 Funk & Wagnall Corporation.

9   T. O. Lloyd, *Empire to Welfare State, English history 1906-1967*, Oxford University Press, 1970, p. 404.

10   Ibid.

11   Copyright © 1999 Roberto Rivera. All rights reserved. International copyright secured. As quoted on 'Focus on the Family' Web Page, 20 July 2000.

12   Peter Schwartz, *21 Century Earth*, Opposing Viewpoints Series, San Diego: Greenhaven Press, Inc, 1996, p. 53. Quote taken from US Bureau of the Census, *Children's Well-Being: an International Comparison*, 1991.

13   Ibid. p. 52.

14   Ibid. p. 56.

15   Ibid. p. 53.

16   Francis Schaeffer, *Trilogy*, Leicester: Inter-Varsity Press, 1990, p. 145.

17   Joseph Wapner, 'My most important decision', *Saturday Evening Post*, July/August 1988, p. 30.

Chapter 7

THE CULTURE OF DEATH

Overview: In this chapter we consider the vital link between abortion and euthanasia, and the predicament older patients face as medical ethicists put quality of life before sanctity of life. This chapter is broken into two sections:

- dealing with abortion.
- dealing with the link between abortion and euthanasia.

The 'To do' activity follows Section 2.

Section 1: Abortion

The culture of death

Many medical ethicists believe that killing a foetus is a humane way of dealing with unwanted pregnancies.[1] In the light of this, it is significant that Pope John Paul II has called ours the 'Culture of Death'. Quite simply, a culture of death is a civilisation that regards killing as a solution to societal problems. The time has come to speak in defence of the unborn because there is a strong correlation between how we treat the unborn – certainly the weakest members of our society – and how we treat other vulnerable members of society, in particular the elderly.

The medium is the message

More than half a century after the genocide of European Jews, people still ask how we allowed this to happen? To better understand the events that came about between 1936 and 1945 in Germany and Eastern Europe (what we now call the Holocaust), we must remember that the atrocities began gradually through laws created by the Nazi party, until the persecution snowballed into the Final Solution, which took the lives of six million human beings.

How could people be so blind to the horror of the Holocaust? Why didn't they do something to stop the killing? Simple – the Nazis controlled the media.

Marshall McLuhan's *The Medium is the Message* (London: Penguin, 1967), Vance Packard's *Hidden Persuaders* (London: Penguin, 1981), and thousands of recent scholarly reports from Britain, Australia, Canada and the USA attest to the awesome influence of mass media on a culture's mind and values – influences so powerful that under Hitler, Nazis across Eastern Europe were able to pass into law draconian ordinances which defied logic, devastated civil liberties, and eventually caused otherwise reasonable people to believe that Jews (and other non-Aryans) were not fit to be called human.

Likewise, by politicising the issue of a woman's so-called personal freedom, pro-abortion proponents have convinced MPs and Lords that unborn babies are not human and therefore merit no human rights. Politicians aside, why do so many ordinary people accept this illogical position? Unfortunately, the media are on the side of 'personal freedom'.

Just prior to the 1997 General Election, the BBC, Channel 4, Channel 5 and ITV insisted that an anti-abortion film be censored before they would air it. The reason? Two minutes and 13 seconds of scenes depicting an abortion complete with the discarded limbs, broken bones and blood unceremoniously dumped into a dustbin: 'It's too offensive', cried the network bosses. Curious – you can see murder, rape, graphic sexual acts, and worse on television, but you can't see a so-called 'simple operation' which occurs every day in our hospitals!

The media are not alone in fostering a culture of death. The women's movement, politicians of all persuasions, educators and some Christians believe abortion should be a matter of choice.

Is an unborn baby human?

Many believe that an unborn baby is not a human being, merely a blob of enzymes and cells. But today, doctors may examine life inside the womb and so they know that the entire chromosomal make-up of a person is established at conception. By three weeks after conception the heart is beating, by six weeks the brain waves can be detected, and the unborn child is recognisable to the eye as a miniature baby by the ninth week. [2]

Anyone with Internet access can see a 12-week-old foetus playing in its mother's womb on the website of the Australian Right to Life Association: http://www.actrtla.org.au

Does an unborn child feel pain?

Most people assume that abortions are a humanitarian way of eliminating an unwanted pregnancy since the baby feels no pain. Nothing could be further from the truth. Peter McCullagh, a Senior Fellow in Developmental Physiology at the John Curtin School of Medical Research, Canberra, has said, 'those anatomical structures subserving the appreciation of pain . . . are present and functioning before the tenth week of life'.[3] That means that the baby feels the abortionist's razor-sharp blades and high-pressure sucking devices every bit as much as the Jews who were tortured, starved, gassed or shot to death by the Nazis. Because medical experts know this, resuscitation equipment is compulsorily available at all abortion clinics, so that, should a foetus manage to survive the effort to terminate it, then every effort can be made to save its life. The recent call by Professor Yvette Glover to anaesthetise unborn babies before aborting them (lest they suffer) is what columnist Mary Kenny calls 'a metaphor of the contradictions which prevail'.[4]

Can the unborn think?

Yes. In fact, unborn babies learn to recognise their mother tongue in the womb, according to Todd Bailey, a psychologist at Cardiff University. His research indicates that babies are even capable of learning speech patterns in the womb. Because abortion has been politicised by special-interest groups, the media and most medical practitioners involved in abortion are not going to make this information widely available.

Legal murder

I am convinced that someday abortion will be seen as a crime against humanity. This is the official stand of the Orthodox and Roman Catholic Churches, as well as of millions of Protestants, Jews, Muslims, Hindus and Sikhs, and scores of prominent medical ethicists and many human rights groups.

Apart from those groups who use abortion as a political football, I believe most people who advocate the use of abortion act out of sincere but flawed humanitarian motives. And as with all flawed motives, serious repercussions are bound to follow.

The domino effect

As a university student back in the 'seventies, I heard a visiting ethics professor predict that the legalisation of abortion and genetic experimentation on foetuses would lead to an ultra-materialistic society where who lives and who dies would be determined not by their intrinsic worth as human beings, for such values will have been swept aside, but by their ability to be happy and productive. In other words, birthright would be determined by the factors having the greatest positive effect on the greatest number of people. He warned gravely that he had already seen this happening in other countries where the politically outré, the poor, the infirm, women, children and most often the elderly, were the victims of such utilitarian realities.[5] He warned that the same could happen here unless we were careful to uphold the sanctity of life.

I dismissed the professor's warning. 'Of course, such things could happen in non-western nations facing harsh economic problems,' I thought, 'but surely it could never happen in a western democracy.' That wasn't even thirty years ago. It is appalling that western values have changed so quickly: ours is the first generation to legalise murder. Our ethics are so perverse that people making a stand for the sanctity of life are seen as suspect, even dangerous.

When abortion was legalised, the high premium our culture once had placed on human life was knocked over domino-style by utilitarianism and relativistic ethics. The visiting professor was correct. Today, not only the unborn but also the infirm and the poor are viewed less as people with the right to live and more as problems to be eliminated.[6]

In the light of the medical evidence that life begins as early as conception, we are no better than the people who looked on silently as millions of humans were legally slaughtered during the Holocaust. Our cruelty is staggering, and as I will show in the next section of this chapter, our cruelty is being directed towards another vulnerable segment of our society – the elderly.

Section 2: Euthanasia

Euthanasia is a Greek word meaning good death. There are two kinds of euthanasia, passive and active. Passive euthanasia occurs when food, medical treatment or other essentials necessary for sustaining life are withheld from a patient for one reason or another. Active euthanasia occurs when a doctor or some other person kills a patient outright. The British Voluntary Euthanasia Society (VES) aims to make it legal for a competent adult, who is suffering unbearably from an incurable illness, to receive medical help to die at his or her own 'considered and persistent request'. They only support voluntary euthanasia in these particular circumstances and only at the patient's competent request.

> *(Some) opposition to voluntary euthanasia focuses on the idea of the 'slippery slope'. This theory states that legalising voluntary euthanasia for those who are incurably ill and ask for help in dying would inevitably lead to other types of euthanasia. That is, society would soon sanction the killing of people against their will. There is no evidence for such an argument – it is unfounded speculation. Voluntary euthanasia – helping a patient to die at their own considered request – is a world away from the murder of vulnerable people.*

The VES also states:

> *Whilst palliative care makes a great difference to many people, it is not the solution for all. Some terminal pain and other distressing symptoms cannot be fully controlled, even with the best care. However, it is quality of life, rather than pain, that is often the main reason behind a patient's request for help in dying. Why should we force someone to live the last days or weeks of their life in a way which, to them, is undignified? Voluntary euthanasia is, above all, about personal choice.* [7]

Despite the talk about choice, many doctors flout the laws and, as I will show, seem willing to disregard the wishes of the patients and their families. One would have to be very naive to think these same doctors would obey future laws designed to protect sick people who are not ready to die once euthanasia is legalised. This ought to set off warning bells. We must speak out against what is going on in our hospitals, for if we do nothing now, it is likely young people today will become the victims of euthanasia when they themselves are elderly. Consider the warning of theologian Martin Niemoller who wrote about the Nazi Gestapo:

(They) came first for the Communists, and I didn't speak up because I wasn't a Communist. Then they came for the Jews, and I didn't speak up because I wasn't a Jew. Then they came for the trade unionists, and I didn't speak up because I wasn't a trade unionist. Then they came for the Catholics, and I didn't speak up because I was a Protestant. Then they came for me, and by that time, there was no one left to speak up. [8]

Active euthanasia could never happen here, you say? Think again. According to the VES:

Euthanasia goes on already. At the moment, the law and current medical practice do not match up. In 1994 a survey published in the British Medical Journal showed that some doctors already help patients to die. Few doctors have been prosecuted and, like Dr Cox, who was convicted of attempted murder in 1992, they have always been treated with great sympathy. Doctors are also legally able to give pain-relieving treatment in such high doses that people may die more quickly. This is known as the 'double effect' – relieving the patient's suffering is the accepted consequence of such treatment, with death as an unintended outcome. [9]

Does euthanasia occur in our hospitals today?

Euthanasia is illegal in the United Kingdom. However, this does not mean that euthanasia does not occur in NHS hospitals. Malcolm Muggeridge, a tireless critic of euthanasia here and abroad, made a comment during a lecture in London in the 1970s which gave British people reason to worry about passive euthanasia being implemented against their will:

(I am) someone who has lived for some years in what I call the NTBR belt, that is to say, belonging to the category of people 65 years and over, who in our humane society are liable to have marked on their medical cards, if they get ill and go into hospital, NTBR, which means 'Not To Be Resuscitated'. [10]

Muggeridge cited cases of the elderly rich flocking to private hospitals to be looked after. The ones run by the Roman Catholic nuns have the longest waiting lists, he said,

not so much because the prospective inmates are particularly pious,(but) because they want to be sure that some zealot for mercy killing will not finish them off arbitrarily by administering excessive sedation; or, if they happened to be in need of an iron lung or attached to a kidney machine, by pulling the plug, as put in today's rather disgusting medical jargon. [11]

Critics ignored Muggeridge, saying he was exaggerating, so the matter was never seriously investigated. But an April 2000 medical report proved Muggeridge was correct about NHS hospitals: Do not resuscitate (DNR) orders were discovered by Age Concern. The nation's media reported that 67-year-old Janet Baker, who had stomach cancer, found the DNR order in her medical notes. She was in hospital being treated for an infection. Her son told how he had twice stopped DNR orders being added to his mother's hospital notes against her wishes. Ministers said they were shocked about such orders, often put there by junior doctors without consultation with the patient or the family and against their wishes.

Thankfully, euthanasia is still illegal here. Moreover, there are laws in place to prevent abuses but, as we have seen, abuses do occur.

The Society for the Protection of Unborn Children (SPUC) has recently condemned the Government's proposals for making decisions on behalf of mentally incapacitated adults as seeking to introduce euthanasia by deception (the Tony Bland judgement). A spokesperson for the society commented:

> *These proposals contain much that is welcome and positive about caring for adults with incapacity. But the Government are deliberately trying to pull the wool over the public's eyes by stating they are opposed to introducing euthanasia into this country while at the same time putting forward proposals which would allow our doctors to withdraw life sustaining food and water from a patient who is not dying. Even worse, however, the Government proposals would give unscrupulous 'proxy decision makers' the power to refuse medical treatment as well as food and fluids on behalf of the sick, elderly and disabled.*
>
> *Although the Government has said it is not 'appropriate to legislate at the present time' to give statutory force to advance statements (living wills), it is a concession which flatters to deceive. The other measures included in this policy statement make this apparent concession meaningless.*
>
> *By giving statutory force to the Tony Bland judgement, which determined that assisted food and fluids are medical treatment, the Government will give those who support euthanasia one of their most cherished goals and put onto the statute book the deliberate ending of life.* [12]

Euthanasia will become legal when the law officially recognises quality of life, not sanctity of life, as the ultimate factor controlling who lives and who dies.

It must be acknowledged that in countries where people provide for their own medical care privately, as many do here in the United Kingdom, there is the possibility that unscrupulous medical practitioners may prolong life artificially. Such doctors wish to extract as much money as possible from families by keeping the patient's vital life signs on the go, knowing that there is no possibility of the patient's survival. To allow a patient in this position to die with compassion and dignity is not euthanasia; it is merely allowing nature to run its course without interference from human beings.

Are older patients actually discriminated against in NHS hospitals?

Euthanasia aside, are older patients actually discriminated against in NHS hospitals? It really depends on which hospital you are talking about. While many hospitals do an exemplary job in geriatrics, others fall far short when it comes to caring for the elderly. During the spring and summer of 2000, Britain's broadsheets all carried compelling accounts of outright age discrimination.

An Age Concern report stated that most family doctors in England believe that elderly patients suffer age discrimination in the National Health Service and almost half said that they would worry if an elderly member of their family was admitted to hospital. GPs told Age Concern of age-based rationing for many kinds of treatments, including cancer treatments, certain drugs, cataract and hip replacement operations. They also said that heart bypass surgery, kidney dialysis and admission to intensive therapy units were also subject to upper age limits.

According to Age Concern, there is overwhelming evidence that the NHS discriminates against older people. A 1999 Age Concern/Gallup survey showed that one in 20 people over 65 has been refused treatment, while one in ten has been treated differently since the age of 50.

Older people report discrimination at all levels of the health service from primary care through to hospitals. It is often explicit, such as when patients are told that a treatment is unavailable to them because of their age. This includes 40 per cent of coronary care units attaching age restrictions to the use of clot-busting drug therapy, the refusal of kidney dialysis or transplants to 66 per cent of kidney patients aged 70 to 79, and no invitations to breast screening for women aged 65 and over.

The discrimination can also be implicit such as when older people are given a low priority by the NHS or experience poor levels of care. This includes delays in hip replacements, the withdrawal of chiropody services which makes many older people housebound, and the often inappropriate use of anti-psychotic drugs in care homes. Many older people also report negative attitudes from NHS staff, which can deny them access to services and the quality of care expected by younger people.

In summary, this report concludes that despite Government assurances of equal treatment, discrimination against older people is widespread within the NHS. For example, Joyce Morgan is a former nurse, diagnostic radiographer and social worker. She says, 'I have met too many old people who almost apologise for being alive . . . Old people are not being treated as equals. They just seem to be in the way.

A Glasgow University study reinforces these ageist attitudes and states that physicians, nurses and radiographers at a Scottish cancer centre regarded old people as a social problem. The study which questioned NHS staff about their attitudes, also stated that the over-65s were under-represented in clinical cancer trials. Of course, once the facts were laid bare the Government took steps to address adverse public reaction. Strict new guidelines to deal with controversial 'do not resuscitate' instructions are being ordered by the Government today to stamp out ageism in NHS hospitals. All NHS trusts will be required to limit the order to four circumstances:

- If the patient's condition means that resuscitation is unlikely to be successful;

- If a mentally competent patient has consistently stated and recorded the fact that he or she wishes not to be resuscitated;

- If an advance directive or living will states that the patient does not want to be resuscitated;

- If successful resuscitation is likely to lead to a quality of life that would not be in the patient's best interests.

   A closer look at the last point shows that medical practitioners are still the ones to determine who lives and who dies, based on a patient's 'quality of life' and economic factors. In other words, nothing has changed.

A two-edged sword

With each life we extinguish, we're wielding a well-honed, double-edged sword. With a forward stroke, we seem to be eliminating an unwanted pregnancy or a painful and useless life; but with the return stroke, we're seriously undermining the value of human life. Moreover, abortion and euthanasia never treat the causes only the symptoms of societal problems. I believe that with the legalising of abortion in 1967, we unwisely crossed a time-honoured taboo. The result is that the once high value placed on human life by society has been radically devalued. We are declaring that the ultimate worth of human life is measured by political, economic or so-called quality-of-life criteria. This pragmatic approach to life reflects perfectly what Pope John Paul II means when he says ours is the Culture of Death.

In his message to the UN's World Assembly on Ageing, Pope John Paul II affirmed: 'Life is a gift of God to man who is created out of love in the image and likeness of God. It is impossible to truly value the life of an older person if the life of a child is not valued from the moment of its conception. No one knows where we might arrive, if life is no longer respected as something inalienable and sacred.' [13]

To consider

The killing of the unborn needs to be put into perspective. Over the past 34 years there have been nearly six million abortions in the UK, roughly the same number of Jews killed in the Holocaust.

How many of these operations were actually performed according to the narrow dictates of the Abortion Act? In 1996, there were 177,225 abortions in England and Wales. [14] That same year, only 2,612 abortions were performed for medical reasons, with a mere three done in emergency to save the mother's life, and none in emergency to prevent grave permanent injury to the mother.

An additional 2,471 abortions were performed as a matter of course to prevent permanent injury to the mothers, despite evidence that the deliberate destruction of the unborn child is never necessary as a medical treatment. [15] Who then had the remaining 172,139 abortions in that year? Needy women deserving protection from back-street abortionists, as the pro-abortionists would have us believe? On the contrary. Government statistics show that most abortions are performed in the wealthier suburbs of the south-east for social reasons. [16]

Unless we return to the belief that life is intrinsically sacred no matter what the age or quality of that life and regardless of the prevailing economic factors that affect that life, hundreds of thousands more innocent people will be murdered each year.

Consider the following oddity: It is no secret that the NHS is short of money and beds. Our hospitals routinely turn away sick elderly patients due to funding shortages, yet they have never turned away someone wanting an abortion due to insufficient funding. In fact, according to Jeremy Laurance, a *Times* health service correspondent, as the demand for abortions increases, senior NHS staff divert funds from other areas to pay for them.[17] As a result, many elderly people are allowed to die in order to save money to kill unborn babies. Moreover, as we age, we ourselves will surely be put at risk of being exploited, manipulated and even disposed of by the younger, productive segment of society.

To do

Remember the media and most medical practitioners are not going to make this information widely available. If they do, they will defend the practices because of their ideological commitment to personal freedom. It is up to the Church to act in defence of the defenceless before the situation degenerates further. What may we do?

- Consider joining the Society for the Protection of Unborn Children (SPUC).

   ### Aims and Objectives
   The Society was formed in Great Britain in January 1967 to rally opposition to the Abortion Bill then being debated in Parliament. Following its enactment as the 1967 Abortion Act, the Society maintains its fundamental opposition to that Act. The principal aim of the Society is to affirm, defend and promote the existence and value of human life from the moment of conception, and to defend and protect human life generally. You may contact SPUC at:

   SPUC
   Phyllis Bowman House
   5/6 St Matthew's Street
   London SW1P 2JT

   Tel: 020 72225845

   Or you may visit its website at http://www.spuc.org.uk/ or, for a comprehensive listing of organisations which support the sanctity of life, check out this website: http://www.prolifeinfo.org/infonet.html

- We have no right to criticise people who support abortion if we refuse to get involved with the needy. To their credit, the people who support the use of death as a means of coping with societal ills are acting out of what they consider to be humanitarian motives. However, I suggest that Christian communities should become havens where needy women may find non-judgemental support as an alternative to having an abortion. To this end, Christians must offer to adopt unwanted children as an alternative to abortion. Many churches already assist pregnant women facing a crisis; but more needs to be done if Christians hope to make a significant impact on a society that believes abortion is the only solution to an unwanted pregnancy.

• Write to your MPs to let them know you are against abortion on demand, and euthanasia, including Living Wills and any other strategy to end life prematurely. Here are two excellent websites to help you become more active in the political process:

http://www.psr.keele.ac.uk/area/uk.htm

http://www.psr.keele.ac.uk/area/uk/eu.htm

• Or write to your MP or Peer at:

The House of Commons/The House of Lords
Westminster
London
SW1A 0PW

• Or write directly to the prime minister at:

The Prime Minister
10 Downing Street
London
SW1A 2AA

• Finally, it's no good simply to call on the Government to 'do something' about euthanasia. The time has come for the Church to take the lead. Dame Cicely Saunders was in her middle years when she began her most important work for humanity and God. Though she is credited with beginning the modern hospice movement, Dame Cicely Saunders has said that that honour really belongs to a Jewish man named David Tasma who died of inoperable cancer in 1947 when he was 40 years old. She visited him often during the two months that he was dying in a very busy surgical ward. After Tasma's death, Dr Saunders volunteered for several years at St Luke's hospital where she saw dying cancer patients being treated for the pain of terminal illness. She studied medicine in order to learn more about pain management, which helped her formulate ideas about caring for the terminally ill. In 1967, nineteen years after David Tasma's death, Cicely Saunders opened St Christopher's hospice in London.[18]

The hospice movement with its emphasis on dignity, respect and its remarkable work in palliative care should make the need for euthanasia redundant. Death with dignity is an ancient Christian concept that has been highjacked by secularists. Would you or members in your church consider doing what Cicely Saunders has done? If not, why not?

References

1   This is the official position of the NHS and the BMA.

2   Information supplied by Brendan Gerard, Society for the Protection of the Unborn Child (SPUC), and printed in the article 'Will the slaughter of the innocents postpone revival?' Michael Apichella, *Renewal*, October 1999, p. 17.

3   Material supplied by the Society for the Protection of the Unborn Child (SPUC).

4   Mary Kenny, The *Sunday Telegraph*, Opinion, http://www.Sundaytelegraph.com/opinion *Electronic Telegraph*, 17 September 2000, issue 2049.

5   For a powerful example of a society that routinely cast out babies and the elderly because of utilitarian and economic factors, see anthropologist Colin Turnbull's *The Mountain People* (Simon and Schuster, 1972), ISBN 0671640984. One reviewer said of the book: 'I found his comparisons between the Ik (a Ugandan tribe) and our own society to be very provocative and insightful. Perhaps we are not so compassionate as we say we are . . .' Source: http://www.amazon.co.uk

6   Anti-abortion groups have condemned a report by two American academics that links the legalising of abortion in 1973 to a drop in crime twenty years later.

    It suggests that abortions performed on poor women reduces the number of unwanted children in lower economic groups, who are the most likely to turn criminal as young adults. University professors Steve Levitt and John Donohue say their study, *Legalised Abortion and Crime*, is not intended as a justification for abortion but is simply an examination of the factors involved in crime reduction.

    The study says many women in the 1970s whose children would have been most likely to commit crimes chose abortions. Therefore, many who would have become criminals in the 1990s were not born.

    Judie Brown, president of the anti-abortion American Life League, said: 'The con-clusions of this study appear to be wedded to the eugenicist theory that equates poverty with undesirable human beings. Any study that predicts the actions of a future generation based solely on the living conditions of their parents is flawed, suggests a racist attitude and should be flatly ignored.'

Joseph Scheidler, executive director of the Pro-Life Action League, said: 'This is the most insidious rationale I have ever heard for tolerating abortion. Naturally if you kill off a million and a half people a year, a few criminals will be in that number.' 'Pro-life groups attack abortion and crime link' by Philip Delves Broughton in New York. Posted on *Electronic Telegraph*.

7   http://www.ves.org.uk/

8   Quoted by Charles Colson in *Kingdoms in Conflict*, Grand Rapids: Zondervan, USA, 1987, p. 125.

9   http://www.ves.org.uk/ Online, 7 September 2000.

10   Malcolm Muggeridge, *Christ and the Media*, Grand Rapids: Eerdmans, USA, 1978, pp. 43-44.

11   Malcolm Muggeridge, *Conversion – A Spiritual Journey*, p. 143.

12   'Euthanasia by deception', SPUC News Release, 27 October 1999, http://www.spuc.org.uk/makingd.htm

13   *The Dignity of Older People and Their Mission in the Church and the World*, Catholic Truth Society, 1999, p. 12.

14   'Abortion too easy, say most women', The *Sunday Telegraph*, 26 October 1997, p. 1.

15   Abortion Statistics http://www.binternet.com/~Devans_23/abstats.htm [online 27 May 1999]

16   Rob Warner, *The Ten Commandments and the Decline of the West*, Kingsway, p. 117.

17   'NHS abortions rise as managers take control', *The Times*, Tuesday, 3 January 1995.

18   'What is in your mind and in your heart: The story of Dame Cicely Saunders, MD' Copyright © 2000 *Women in Medicine* ® – info@womeninmedicine.com

Chapter 8

THE ROLE OF THE MEDIA

Up to now, we have been considering the divide between the older and younger generations. Now let's examine a contributing factor to the divide – the mass media and its role in shaping society's attitudes and values towards the elderly.

The United Nations declared 1999 as the International Year of Older Persons, and during that year it commissioned a study into perceptions and portrayals of older people. Volunteers monitored the media for a period of one week. The findings were not favourable. Seniors are either victims or eccentric. The data was gleaned from a total of 3,686 references to older people and older people's issues.

> The conclusions reached were that . . . there are stories in abundance about older people and issues . . . but unfortunately they are depicted as 'victims' – especially where crime is concerned – a generalisation that ignores the way in which many older people live and reinforces the fear that older people themselves harbour of being victims of crime. (With a few rare exceptions) most seniors are portrayed as frail objects of pity. [1]

Stories about ageing issues were rare in the national newspapers, with the one exception of NHS stories. During the period under review there was only one relevant headline in the national daily broadsheets, but none in the tabloids, national Sunday broadsheets or Sunday pages in English local and regional papers and a scant two per cent of the total audited coverage of seniors was felt to merit a prominent headline. [2]

Despite the many accomplishments of the elderly today and throughout history, seniors are still stereotyped in our media as seedy, forgetful, or odd.

There will never be harmony between the generations as long as the media misrepresents the elderly, for the media plays a vital role in forming societal attitudes. If people are unhappy with how the elderly are portrayed in the media, but they remain silent about it, they have no right to complain. But what can be done?

Here are four suggestions:

1 Political coalitions

We may form a political voice consisting of anyone else interested in issues pertaining to the elderly. Collectively, we must tell Parliament of our views. This would encourage legislators to make more informed decisions about laws that govern media fare, particularly as it relates to the portrayal of the elderly and issues of importance to them.

Some argue that the Government won't respond to pressure groups. But political coalitions are an effective means of bringing about legislative change. Years ago Blacks and Asians were routinely stereotyped in the media until concerned people put pressure on society to enact laws that prevent negative racial stereotyping. Christians have only just recently discovered the power of the democratic process. During the summer of 2000, people who favour a biblical attitude towards homosexuals won the battle over the repeal of Section 28. According to Baroness Young who led the fight to maintain Section 28, the crucial vote was won because of Christians putting pen to paper.

Writing in the *Guardian*, Kamal Ahmed states that Baroness Young told of the flood of well-reasoned letters that had an enormous influence on the majority vote to retain the clause. According to Young, 'letters do count'.

Ahmed went on to say of the Christians who were motivated to write:

> *These are the new Christian soldiers – well organised, well funded, disciplined and committed groups of people who have assiduously courted those in power. Last week saw their political high point – the emphatic Lords defeat of government proposals to repeal Section 28. The campaign was led by Baroness Young, who has close links with Care and two other leading religious groups that have built themselves into formidable lobbying organisations – the Christian Institute and Family and Youth Concern.* [3]

If Christians don't organise and send a clear message to Parliament, we can't blame it for allowing the elderly to be misrepresented in the media.

2 Strategic viewing

The media works on the basis of supply and demand. Programme makers and editors know who their audiences are, and they want to keep them. Many are unaware of the demand for programming which respects the elderly. Therefore Christians must make their viewing habits known. By using the *Radio Times*, *Cross Rhythms* and other guides to media fare, families may begin planning their weekly viewing, listening or reading, thereby boosting the ratings of the features they most enjoy. Once it becomes clear that certain productions draw substantial audiences, then more of the same will follow.

3 Media awareness

Get into the habit of noting the names of the people responsible for programming or publications and fire off a letter, fax, e-mail or phone call to make your opinion known. Gripe about what you hate; applaud what you like. Producers and editors do respond to informed feedback; complaints are taken seriously. Radio critic Matt Born reported that radio listeners were switching off in record numbers in protest about offensive material. A third of those who had been offended had turned off and a third tuned into another station. A report published jointly by the Radio Authority and Broadcasting Standards Commission said that listeners were more willing to retune in search of 'quality'. Stephen Whittle, director of the commission, expressed the hope that the findings would encourage radio stations to ensure that basic human values of respect and dignity would continue to be an important part of radio output.

4 Media participation

Once upon a time, Christians dominated the media, making no apology for their faith. They didn't have to. Their work was every bit as good as – and some would say better than – their non-believing contemporaries. Over the years, such people made the effort to bring young people under the influence of the Holy Spirit, not the spirit of the world.[4] Consider Lord John Reith, the first General Manager of the BBC and a committed Christian.

Under Reith's tenure the BBC made programmes that cultivated proper respect for the elderly. One crucial aspect of Reith's policies was children's programming. Reith understood that the future of British culture was its children, so he took great pains to ensure the highest quality programming for this segment of the audience. This responsibility was delegated to the highly capable Mrs Ella Fitzgerald (who later pioneered *Women's Hour*, still broadcast today on Radio 4). She was assisted by, among others, Arthur Burrows who wrote, 'there is no section of our programme work upon which more time and thought is spent than that termed the Children's Hour.' But that was then. This is now. It is worthwhile to note how today's BBC's policies contrast John Reith's.

Janet Street-Porter, the former BBC television 'youth expert', colourfully summed up current BBC children's programming policy by stating that there were just a few key things in finding a youth policy. One of these was that there *had* to be a generation divide; if a parent came into the room and said to the child, 'What the hell is that rubbish you're watching?' you knew you were on to a winner. Note the intentional attempt to divide the generations.

At the time, columnist Mary Kenny reported that Janet Street-Porter had been attacked by Family and Youth Concern, a body of concerned citizens worried about Britain's sinking levels of taste and decency. Its publication, *Family Bulletin*, questioned Ms Street-Porter's suitability. She had been married and divorced three times and was childless by choice, and yet she filled a job which specifically called for dealing with children's media fare; she also apparently deliberately set out to alienate youngsters from their parents.

Mary Kenny pointed out that Janet herself admitted that her desired goal was to turn youngsters against their parents' tastes. Although the BBC claims all the high-minded independence that John Reith bestowed upon it, it is none the less rejecting almost all of Reith's impeccable ethics. Today Janet Street-Porter is a mere footnote in BBC youth programming, but sadly her policy lives on with a vengeance.

Today's media icons for millions of teenage girls (and boys) are epitomised by Zoë Ball. In 1998, Zoë Ball was presenting a Saturday morning children's TV programme as well as presenting a BBC Radio 1 programme. At the time, Ms Ball blithely informed media correspondent Jan Moir that she had a love affair going with Jack Daniels (a brand of American whisky) and bragged about how she had recently been drunk for three days and had to present her programme, *Live and Kicking*, with far too much alcohol in her system.

As if appearing drunk on TV before the nation's under-12s is not bad enough, she also had the youth audience by the ears as co-presenter of BBC Radio 1's weekday 'Breakfast Show'. Her formula for good radio? In the words of one radio critic, 'I do wish she would stop going on about her knickers.'

Some would say that kids are smart enough not to be influenced by people like Zoë Ball. I wish that were so. Parents please note, in a national magazine poll, Zoë Ball was voted the personality 86 per cent of teenage girls most related to. Although Zoë Ball has gone, her replacement, ex-model Sara Cox, is in the same Ball and Street-Porter mould. This means when it comes to role models, the media will have greater influence over your children's attitudes than you will.

I've already mentioned the United Nations study into perceptions and portrayals of older people; the study has shown that the elderly are routinely denigrated in our media. Today, the media is the exclusive domain of talented but misguided secularists who refuse to follow the biblical mandate to honour the elders in our midst. I wonder what the media's image of the elderly would be like if committed Christians were given the jobs of developing children's media fare for the BBC and ITV and the myriad new cable networks.

Of course, we cannot blame secular minds for having a low view of the elderly; we have only ourselves and the Church to blame. Where are the Christian communicators today? Would your church support a person trying to make a difference in the media? The churches of this country support hundreds of missionaries who go overseas to spread the gospel. But these same churches seem not to grasp that Britain has become a needy mission field thanks to fifty years of unfettered secular humanism. Christians need to reclaim radio, television, print, cinema and drama as part of their mission.

Congregations must help their own people become properly trained for the work. Each year the BBC sponsors projects geared to find new faces and voices for tomorrow's programmes. In the summer of 2000, the BBC ran a talent-seeking campaign on breakfast cereal boxes.[5] The advertisement named the cities where the auditions were to be held – London, Glasgow, Manchester and Belfast – and appropriate telephone numbers were supplied. How many youngsters from your congregation applied for this opportunity to influence the media? Pray that God would inspire godly youngsters to take the Gospel to the nation through the media. The need is always there for new talent. Check out the BBC's own talent-seeking website at http://www.bbc.co.uk/talent

Also have a look at http://www.bbc.co.uk/writersroom/index for guidance on how to break into writing for the media. The *Guardian's* media section carries ads inviting young people to apply for places in BBC radio, TV and other media. Why not use that page as the way forward for a career in media?

As Charles Colson has said, Christian conversion is not merely personal; we are called to transform the culture around us as well. This means the arts and mass media must be seen as a legitimate mission field for all Christians. Until this happens, we may expect the elderly to be the butt of the younger generation's jokes.

To consider

Would your church support people trying to make a difference in mass media? The churches of this country need to view radio, television, print, cinema and drama as an integral part of their mission. To do so, they must recruit those in their midst with the aptitude and the desire to work in the media.

A few churches already do this. One of the best examples that I know of is the Berkshire, Buckinghamshire and Oxfordshire Churches' Media Trust (CMT), a charitable trust that supports Christians working in the media. Originally set up to encourage Christians in local broadcasting, CMT is fully ecumenical and seeks to promote excellence in media relations for churches and church leaders by raising the profile of print, broadcast and electronic media for churches and making the churches visible in the media.'

Since it was established in 1991, CMT has:

- funded a religious production post for BBC Radio Oxford and another for BBC Radio Berkshire
- helped fund Christian contributions to independent local radio stations in High Wycombe (1170) and Aylesbury (Mix 96)
- provided funding for a 'Care Desk' at Fox FM in Oxford
- provided equipment for a number of local church Restricted Service Licence (RSL) special event radio stations
- made numerous small grants for media related projects.

Finally, here are some disturbing findings:

In 1994, Professor Elizabeth Newson of Nottingham University published a report 'Video violence and the protection of children', which looks at the effects of screen violence. 'Video violence and the protection of children' was the first report to acknowledge that what children watch has an influence on their behaviour; findings that have since been reinforced by several other studies. More than twenty-five leading psychologists have endorsed Professor Newson's findings.

It has been found that:

• the critical period of exposure to television is pre-adolescent childhood. (American Academy of Paediatrics)

• studies conclude that viewing certain programmes '. . . can increase aggression in children, make them more fearful and less trusting, and desensitise them to violent behaviour by other people'. (National TV Violence Study)[6]

• according to an article in the June 1994 issue of *Psychology Digest*, a definite correlation has been established between the growing violence on television and in movies and the increase in aggressive behaviour of people in general, but especially in the young.[7]

Few people dispute the above facts. Since this is so, I suggest that there may be a link between the media's general denigration of the elderly and the increase of violent crimes against the elderly.

Mass media is a powerful tool for helping to form a culture's values. Since the 1960s many thoughtful and thought-provoking television programmes and films have devoted their creative powers to fighting racism, child abuse, jingoism, spousal abuse and other social ills. The time has come for ageism to come under fire by serious producers. But who will make these programmes?

To do

It is the Church's responsibility to ensure that qualified Christians work within the media, helping to form the messages that inform the attitudes towards the elderly of this nation. To this end, churches must help Christians become properly trained for media work. Consider committing yourself to praying for these organisations listed below. Perhaps you or your group might consider supporting these organisations financially. Finally, is God calling you to a ministry in the media? Contact one of these organisations and see how they may help you get started in putting Christ back into the media. Remember: if you can't beat the media, join it.

Useful media addresses

The Churches' Media Trust
The Revd Richard Thomas
Diocesan Church House
North Hinksey
Oxford
OX2 0NR

Tel: 01865 208200

Email: thomasrp@thomasrp.demon.co.uk

Association of Christian Writers
73 Lodge Hill Road
Farnham
Surrey
GU10 3RB

Tel: 01252 715746

Email: admin@christianwriters.org.uk

Tamezin Magazine (a magazine produced for and by young people)
1 Chelsea Embankment
London
SW3 4L

Fax: 020 8992 3472

Christian Communications Commission
PO Box 2
Dewsbury
West Yorkshire
WF13 4XG

References

1   *Goodtimes*, 'Seniors still stereotyped?' Association News, April/May 2000, p. 65.

2   Ibid.

3   Kamal Ahmed, 'Onward Christian lobbyists', *Guardian Unlimited* Online, 30 July 2000.

4   *The Cambridge Companion to the Bible* makes a clear distinction between Christians who are under the influence of the Holy Spirit and people who are under the spirit of the world: Of the Christians it states, 'Those who adopt this way of life will experience hatred from the world, which rejected the crucified Christ . . . But by the Holy Spirit, God will guide them, enable them to persevere, and reveal to them the truth about God and his purpose in the world. ('The 'I Am' sayings of Jesus', *The Cambridge Companion to the Bible*, Cambridge University Press, 1997, p. 544-545.)

5   The information was advertised on a package of Kellogg's Corn Flakes in July 2000. The round of auditions ended on 13 August 2000. The campaign is sponsored by Kellogg's, *The Times*, and WH Smith.

6   Source: North Carolina Coalition for Pulling the Plug on Media Violence, via PR NEWSWIRE.

7   *Computer Games, Violence and Children* by Bryan Leech, reprinted from PC Update October 1994, the Journal of Melbourne PC User Group Inc.

Part Three

THE AGE OF DEPENDENCE

Chapter 9

WHEN PARENTS BEGIN TO DECLINE

Overview: This chapter explores what happens when elderly parents begin to decline, and the problems faced by the elderly, such as hypothermia, Alzheimer's disease and stroke. This chapter supplies addresses of agencies that are concerned with caring for the aged and infirm.

The declining years

As children, we depend on our parents physically and emotionally. Although few of us like to think about it, we know they will not live for ever. As the Psalmist writes, 'For all our days pass away under thy wrath, our years come to an end like a sigh' (Psalm 90:9). Although this is a poetic thought, if we examine it in the light of current research on how we age, we will soon discover that it is actually a very scientific observation, rather like the Second Law of Thermodynamics which may be summed up: 'All things in nature tend to wear out gradually.' Since we are a part of nature, we may expect to wear out and eventually die one day. But what do we do when Mum and Dad begin to weaken? As we have seen in previous chapters, the Bible tells us to honour and obey our parents. When their health and minds begin to fail, that's the time the elderly need their children's love the most!

Problems presented by the ailing relative

Role-reversal

Tony and Jan had planned the holiday of a lifetime – an around-the-world trip to Australia via Canada to visit their children and to see their grandchildren in person. This had to be cancelled when Tony's 79-year-old mother slipped and fractured her pelvis. Although Tony's father had died years before, his mother had proved to be self-sufficient, running her small flat, doing her own cooking and cleaning, and even driving her own car. Now she needed help. For Tony and Jan, aged 51, the roles had been reversed: now it was the children who had to look after the parent.

Privately, Jan has admitted that she feels both resentful and guilty. 'I've so looked forward to this time in our lives when we would be able to travel and enjoy the results of our years of hard work; now this had to happen. I just wonder when *my* parents' health is going to go.' Tony worries what might happen to Jan if he dies and she is left on her own in Britain with children in the Far East and America.

We have seen that the number of elderly people in our society is growing. By 2025 it is estimated that there will be 11.5 million people between the ages of 50 and 65, and 19 per cent of the population will be at or beyond retirement age.[1] This means as the number of elderly people increases, more and more middle-aged men and women will face problems similar to Tony and Jan's.

For some families, when a crisis arises, there may be several siblings who are able to share the responsibility of looking after ailing parents. For others, this is not the case. A lack of time, insufficient funds, or great distances prevent them from being of much help. Still others will simply shirk the responsibility. In most cases, whatever the circumstances, the responsibility of having to cope with an infirm elderly relative comes unexpectedly. According to Jan, 'We never thought Tony's Mum would become a problem; she's been so independent.'

Have a plan

All of us ought to be thinking about the general problems associated with ageing as well as ways we can give practical help to people who need assistance when an elderly member of their family sickens and can no longer function alone.

Perhaps some of the problems Tony and Jan now face might have been avoided if they had taken the time to plan what they would do in such an emergency.

When sickness comes, families that are close and live nearby are able to help. This is what happened when octogenarian Alec Bailey of Suffolk lost both his legs and had to have heart surgery in the span of a few years. His daughter-in-law Wanda told me, 'Dad was never a burden to us. I'll never forget how he was always there for us when we were first married. He had a simple Christian faith, and that gave him strength to bear up under all the pain he was in up to his last days.' His son said, 'We took care of Dad ourselves, but we did have help from time to time. But it was Dad's sense of humour and his faith that made the task bearable.' Alec's sense of humour kept everyone laughing, including the medical staff that looked after him. Wanda said, 'Even the consultant and the nurses came to his funeral. But more amazingly, Dad had fought in the Second World War, landing at Normandy in 1944. After the war, he struck up a close friendship with a German prisoner of war here in England. But the two men lost contact after the former POW returned to Germany. To our delight, this man made his way to England from Germany to pay his last respects when he had learned Dad had died.'

Consider a similar case: Like Wanda, Mary was called upon to look after her elderly father-in-law after he had broken his hip. However, unlike Alec, her father-in-law was self-centred, rarely thanking Mary for her services, and he was always quick with a cutting remark or a complaint. Mary knew that this was not going to work out, so she immediately sought help.

Mary told her husband about the situation, and insisted that they both talk it over with trusted friends from their church. This was both tense and awkward for everyone involved, but all sat and listened to Mary without making any judgements. As she talked, Mary suddenly found the courage to admit openly to her husband that she never liked his father. What's more, she felt that he had never liked her, and he was somehow using his condition to punish her. They all agreed there was no use in confronting the old man with any of this. Instead, they decided to take immediate action.

Firstly, they prayed about Mary's attitude towards her father-in-law. They knew Mary's perception of the situation, whether real or imagined, had to change if the problem was to be solved. They also prayed, asking that God would show them the way forward since Mary did not want to turn her back on her father-in-law. Mary's case demonstrates an advantage that Christian counsellors have over secular ones – we may suggest praying about our problems, and we can expect God to help. We can call upon the Holy Spirit to come alongside us as we face seemingly insurmountable situations, giving us grace to be forgiving and patient.

Secondly, they decided Mary simply couldn't go it alone. In the weeks that followed, Mary's father-in-law was still irascible, but the overall situation was much improved because it was agreed that Mary needed time off from her heavy and largely thankless duties. To help her find space in a busy schedule, Clare, a woman in their church, spent one day and one night a week caring for the old man. This was good for him too, because he was seeing a new face and Clare came to him fresh and full of fun and energy. Mary's father-in-law looked forward to her visits.

By admitting her feelings, and by seeking help from her friends, Mary defused a potential time-bomb which could have left lasting psychological and emotional damage to her, her family and friends. In the end, Mary and her father-in-law enjoyed a good relationship until his death.

Many families with elderly relatives may be on the brink of a life-shattering crisis, but rather than face up to the realties, they choose to live in a form of denial. Church leaders need to encourage their congregations to begin talking now about the potential problems associated with ageing parents; congregations must also be ready to offer practical help when a crisis hits.

Attitude: the key to coping

Emotional preparation

Even if you find yourself prepared for a crisis, you should examine your attitudes during the situation. Negative feelings need to be identified and discussed immediately.

When an elderly relative falls ill, younger relatives may feel resentful because their established routines are now upset. They may react to their relative's needs out of a sense of duty rather than love. In addition to creating all sorts of practical problems for the middle-aged relatives, rapidly declining parents remind their children of their own impending demise and ultimately their own deaths. This hits especially hard during middle age, which for many people is already a time of crisis due to regret over lost opportunities, the onset of greying hair and wrinkles, and a host of other physical and psychological complexities.

Dr Kenneth Taylor, translator of the *Living Bible*, wrote in his memoirs of the time when his aged father came to live with him and his family of eleven. A godly man known for his compassion, Kenneth Taylor admits that he bitterly resented his father's presence in his home.

According to Dr Taylor, his father's declining years intersected with some of the hardest years he had faced as a struggling author and translator. Consequently, Dr Taylor became bad-tempered with his family, and he was unable – even unwilling – to empathise with his ailing father. I was very moved by Dr Taylor's candid admission years later that after his father's sudden death, he desperately wished he had shown more love to the man who had given him life and raised him. But by then, it was too late.

Examining our attitudes calls for much soul searching and honesty. If children have had a good relationship with their parents over the years, it's likely that they will find their own ways of looking after ailing relatives. If the opposite is true, however, it may be very difficult until they first sort out and come to terms with their innermost feelings towards their parents. It might be that the crisis is not the actual problem of the parents' failed health; but rather it is the result of long-buried hurts or resentments.

No need to feel guilty

Guilt is the last thing a Christian needs to deal with when coping with ill, elderly relatives. It is a powerful and destructive emotion. When the parent-child role is reversed, it's sometimes hard to suddenly stop being someone's child and start being their primary carer. Commands from unwell parents such as 'Do as I say, I'm still you mother!' are best taken with a grain of salt. The middle-aged children must remember that they themselves are adults at this stage, and the command to obey the parents must be considered in the light of what's actually best for all in the given situation. To give in to every demand is impossible, and in any case, demands are often excessive if not unrealistic. In every situation, we must think objectively. By admitting in advance that there will be some demands which are best ignored, and others which will require great patience and a humble, servant spirit, middle-aged children and their families and friends will be better able to avoid feelings of guilt. For, when it comes down to it, doing what's best for the ailing relative instead of acting irrationally is the way to honour them.

The aged relatives' point of view

A softly-spoken old man has steadily lost weight and developed high blood pressure since his wife of fifty years had a stroke that changed her once sunny disposition into one of perpetual confusion. Choking back the tears, the old man says, 'My wife can't dress herself, can't be trusted alone, can't prepare meals. I told my doctor that I'd give my last penny to make this stop.'

This telling comment reminds us that although this situation is bad for families of ill and aged people, it is beyond description for the elderly ailing person or the spouse. Such a dramatic change in health causes fear and frustration for the elderly as they discover they are not in control of their lives any more.

A common defence mechanism is for one or both of the elderly people to deny that there is a problem. 'Dad insists he can take care of Mother,' said one man. 'But her senility is so bad that more than once she has wandered out to the shops wearing only her nightdress. The truth is, Dad's defeated, but he won't admit it.'

Some ageing parents will try to cope by avoiding situations that underscore their problems. For example: 'Mum refuses to see any visitors because her hearing is going and this upsets her. What she doesn't realise is she is losing her friends because they feel snubbed by her.' Or, 'My Mum is wracked with pain from rheumatism. Dad refuses to allow people from church to come over to help do the laundry or cook meals for them. He stands in the door and smiles, saying everything is under control when in fact, inside it's totally chaotic. When my wife and I drive up there every other week, we find they've been living on tinned sardines and crisps; rubbish is piled up, and the clothes they wear are filthy because the laundry is stacked up to the ceiling. My wife and I spend the whole weekend putting things right, but we can't stay there beyond Sunday, so we know we'll just have to do the same again in a fortnight. The thing is, worried as I am about my mother, I'm more scared that Dad's losing his mind. How else can I explain his crazy behaviour?'

Understanding the behaviour

Many elderly people act strangely because they are simply scared of the new circumstances they now face. The result may be resentment aimed at those around them; dogmatic, inflexible demands placed on family members; or worse, self-destructive behaviour. Remember that when this happens, an elderly person is trying to survive in the way that seems best. Another reason why personality changes so radically is that elderly people are fearful. There are many very real dangers for the elderly such as injury from falling, crime, starvation, and hypothermia.

Hypothermia

For old people who are reasonably fit and healthy, living in homes with central heating, and eating regular nutritious meals, winter cold is a small threat. But for many elderly people in Britain, hypothermia is a potential killer. [2]

Older people must keep warm in winter, especially if they are on the mend from injury or illness. Younger, healthy people react to cold temperatures quickly and efficiently, but coping with the cold is a different story for the elderly if they are unable to move about easily. If they're confined to their beds, they can't put on extra layers of clothing or add extra blankets to their beds. In addition, they can't exercise to warm up; and being in bed in one constant position causes their bodies to become cold, stiff and sore.

Shivering and goose pimples are a reaction that produces warmth in our muscles. In old people, these warming reactions are frequently lessened, or may even be totally absent; therefore, they have little or no natural defence against the extremes of cold weather.

Alzheimer's disease

According to *Newsweek* magazine, medical experts have dubbed Alzheimer's disease 'the disease of the century'. The causes are unknown and the effects are degenerative and irreversible. It strikes people of every ethnic and social background, and it is increasing with the rapid growth of the elderly population in Britain. Many doctors think that the disease is genetically inherited, but there is insufficient data to prove this. Hollywood actress Rita Hayworth, movie producer Otto Preminger, actress Dana Andrews, artist Norman Rockwell and Ronald Reagan, former United States President, were all struck in old age by Alzheimer's disease.

A group of diseases called the dementias cause damage to the brain. This means that the people affected have problems thinking and remembering. The damage dementia causes is progressive. This means that they gradually get worse. Alzheimer's disease is the most common type of dementia. There are other types of dementia that cause similar symptoms. There is no cure for dementia at the moment. However, there are treatments that can help, and many ways that you and others can help the person with dementia enjoy life.

You may find the behaviour of your relative difficult and puzzling at times. It can help if you think about what they might be experiencing. Try to put yourself in their shoes. People with dementia have problems with their memory; they may be able to remember events that happened when they were 6 but not something you said five minutes ago. Don't get impatient with them if they can't remember.

Someone with dementia can also have difficulties talking about what they are feeling or what they would like to do. You might be able to help them by looking at their 'body language' – the expression on their face or the movements of their body. Remember, people with dementia have feelings. You can still show that you care about them.

When someone in the family develops dementia, everyone is affected. But people react to the situation in very different ways.

- You may feel very sad about what is happening to someone you love. You may feel irritated or embarrassed by the person's behaviour.

- You may feel resentful that you are now responsible for someone who used to care for you.

- You may feel angry because the person has changed and other family members seem stressed and have less time for you.

- Try not to bottle up your feelings. Talk to someone close – perhaps a good friend or a member of your family. Or it may help to speak to someone who is not directly involved.

You can speak in confidence to an adviser on the Alzheimer's Helpline. Telephone 0845 300 0336 between 8.30am and 6.30pm. Finding out as much information as possible about the person's illness may help.

Email the Alzheimer's Society for advice at: info@alzheimers.org.uk or phone the Alzheimer's Helpline on 0845 300 0336.

Website: http://www.alzheimers.org.uk/

Questions and answers about stroke [3]
A stroke occurs when blood flow to the brain is interrupted. When a stroke occurs, brain cells in the immediate area begin to die because they no longer receive the oxygen and nutrients they need to function.

What are the types of strokes?
A stroke can occur in two ways. In an ischemic stroke, a blood clot blocks or plugs a blood vessel or artery in the brain. About 80 per cent of all strokes are ischemic. In a haemorrhagic stroke, a blood vessel in the brain breaks and bleeds into the brain. The other 20 percent of strokes are haemorrhagic.

What are the symptoms of stroke?
What makes stroke symptoms distinct is their sudden onset:

- Sudden numbness or weakness of face, arm or leg – especially on one side of the body

- Sudden confusion or trouble speaking or understanding
- Sudden trouble seeing in one or both eyes
- Sudden trouble walking, dizziness, loss of balance or co-ordination
- Sudden severe headache with no known cause.

Why are some victims unable to identify stroke symptoms?

Because stroke injures the brain, one is not able to perceive one's own problems correctly. To a bystander, the stroke patient may seem unaware or confused. A stroke victim's best chance is if someone nearby recognises the stroke and acts quickly.

What should a bystander do?

If you believe someone is having a stroke – if they lose the ability to speak, or move an arm or leg on one side, or experience facial paralysis on one side – call the emergency services immediately. Stroke is a medical emergency. Immediate treatment may save someone's life and enhance his or her chances for successful rehabilitation and recovery.

What are the risk factors for stroke?

- High blood pressure increases your risk of stroke four to six times.
- Heart disease, especially a condition known as atrial fibrillation or AF, can double your risk of stroke.
- Your risk also increases if you smoke, have diabetes, sickle cell disease, high cholesterol, or a family history of stroke.

What can you do to reduce your risk of stroke?

- Monitor your blood pressure
- Track your cholesterol level
- Stop smoking
- Exercise regularly
- Find out if you should be taking a drug to reduce blood clotting.

Stroke Helpline

0845 30 33 100, Local Call Rate (UK)

Website: http://www.stroke.org.uk/

To consider

Most middle-aged children of ailing parents recognise and accept responsibility for their parents, and they love them through their later years. But even for those who have enjoyed a good relationship with their parents, unexpected demands may strain the relationship to breaking point.

The key to coping with a crisis is to think about it before it happens. People with elderly parents must talk through a plan of action in case the health of one or both parents fails. Admittedly, this can be an unpleasant task, but it will be far more unpleasant to try to cope after the life-changing crisis strikes. To put it bluntly, the time to buy insurance is before the accident happens, not after.

If they can afford it, some families put aside a sum of money each month in order to have a fund on hand in case special care is necessary for an ailing relative. Others decide in advance that it would be best if the parents moved in with one of the children. Still others may make arrangements to have one or both of the parents placed in a nursing home. Whatever the decision, by making advance plans, the elderly relatives will have the satisfaction of having their say in a matter that directly affects their lives while they are in good health. Often, what the elderly person has to say on the matter will turn out to be the best advice of all. Everyone involved will be thinking clearly and logically, since important decisions are being made under normal circumstances, free of emotional stress and pressures associated with emergency. Moreover, elderly parents need to know that they are in charge of their own lives; they must be able to make decisions about matters that ultimately affect them. Therefore, the time to be making these all-important plans for the unforeseen future is now.

To do

The Church today needs to recapture the vision that Paul had of the Church. As the Body of Christ, we are an extended family, not a mere stone edifice where people gather briefly once or twice a week for formal services. Ministers and teachers in the churches have the responsibility for ensuring that the congregation understand this obligation so that they may benefit from membership here and now, and not just in the next life. As we encourage our congregation to lend help to those in need, let's not forget that the key to a workable situation is prayer, for prayer has achieved more good than we will ever know in this life.

Finally, when our elderly relatives begin to decline and we are required to help, we must not lose hope. A positive balance of prayer and help from friends will give us, and our ailing elderly relatives, hope and a positive way forward.

Help the Aged is one of the best-known organisations dedicated to helping older people in practical ways. There are all sorts of ways in which you can support them, whether you are looking for ways to fundraise, provide practical support or simply make a donation. For more information contact:

Head Office:
Help the Aged
St James' Walk
Clerkenwell Green
London
EC1R 0BE

Tel: 020 7253 0253
Fax: 020 7250 4474
Email: info@helptheaged.org.uk

Wales Office:
Room 123
CSV House
Williams Way
Cardiff

Email: infocymru@helptheaged.org.uk

Scotland:
Heriot House
Heriot Hill Terrace
Edinburgh
EH7 4DY

Tel: 0131 556 4666
Email: info@helptheaged.org.uk

Northern Ireland:
Ascot House
Shaftesbury Square
Belfast
BT2 7DB

Tel: 028 90 230666
Email: helptheagedni@helptheaged.org.uk

Website: http://www.helptheaged.org.uk/

References

1   Based on census statistics compiled in the 1980s.

2   It is difficult to give an exact figure for the number of people who are affected by hypothermia each year. Hypothermia death figures greatly underestimate the problem of hypothermia and cold-related deaths. Hypothermia is difficult to diagnose and if other illnesses, such as pneumonia and heart disease are present, it is more likely they will be recorded as the main cause of death. However, the figures given below show that in 1997 and 1998, 78% of deaths where hypothermia was mentioned on the death certificate were of people aged 65 or over. Of those over 65 around 64% were aged over 80. It is clear that the risk of hypothermia rises sharply with age (Age Concern, 'Hypothermia death figures and excess winter deaths').

3   Facts taken from the web page of the National Institute of Neurological Disorders and Stroke.
    http://www.ninds.nih.gov/health_and_medical/pubs/stroke_backgrounder.htm

Part Four

THE WAY FORWARD

Chapter 10

FROM HERE TO ETERNITY

Overview: This chapter sheds light on how the churches of Bury St Edmunds are helping to meet the spiritual needs of elderly people in their community.

There is no doubt that secular organisations do a fine job in caring for the needs of the elderly. Having said that, the spiritual needs of the elderly are often overlooked by professional carers. This is where the churches play a vital role.

Geoff Birkby is a member of Bury St Edmunds Churches Together looking at the Care of Older People (CTCOP). He told me, 'As a Christian organisation, we felt it was urgent to gauge the spiritual needs of the elderly in our community, and, more importantly, to discover how the churches may help to meet them.'

The CTCOP research group visited and spoke to local church leaders. Geoff added, 'The aim was to look for good practices which could be shared among the churches in order to enhance attention, and to give more care to the elderly – those within residential care homes and those living in their own homes.'

On the following pages I have summarised their report and its findings to give food for thought for churches eager to serve the elderly more effectively.

Survey of spiritual care of older people

A questionnaire (see page 114) was sent to all participating churches. Once the churches responded, a second questionnaire (see page 115) was sent to residential homes. The results of the research concluded that there is generally good care by the churches in the area covered by CTCOP; however, much depends on the level of commitment of the elderly, the churches and the residential home managers.

QUESTIONNAIRE TO ALL WORSHIPPING COMMUNITIES
(delete yes/no as appropriate)

Name of church _____

1 a Do you hold meetings for over-50s on your premises? _____ (Yes No)

   b If yes, do these include worship? _____ (Yes No)

2 Do you have worshipping members resident in sheltered
   housing/homes or other establishments? _____ (Yes No)

3 Is your community responsible for regular worship for
   over-50s groups off church premises? _____ (Yes No)

4 If answer to question 3 is 'Yes', please answer:

     Where held _____

     How often _____

     Average attendance _____

     Lay led/Minister led/Varies _____

   Does this include:

     Singing? _____ (Yes No)

     Reading/homily? _____ (Yes No)

     Eucharistic prayer? _____ (Yes No)

     Communion? _____ (Yes No)

   When communion is offered, is it open to all? _____ (Yes No)

   Is a musical instrument available? _____ (Yes No)

   Who initiates the service? _____

   Is there a collection? _____ (Yes No)

   If yes, what is the collection for? _____

5 Does your church have spare resources for

     Leading worship? _____ (Yes No)

     Accompanying hymns? _____ (Yes No)

**Thank you for your time in replying;
we hope to keep in contact once the survey is completed.**

QUESTIONNAIRE TO ALL RESIDENTIAL HOMES
(delete yes/no as appropriate)

Name of home _____

Contact _____

Type of home _____

Number of residents _____

Religious services

Do you have any links with local churches? _____ (Yes No)

If the answer is *yes*, please identify these churches:

_____

Do these churches hold services on your premises? _____ (Yes No)

Are these services adequate for the needs of your residents? _____ (Yes No)

If the answer is *no*, do you encourage churches to visit your home? ____ (Yes No)

Do you hold services other than those organised by churches? _____ (Yes No)

Are these services adequate for residents of any denomination? _____ (Yes No)

Please make any comments you wish on any of the services held in your home:

_____

Residents' personal needs

Do you inform local or linked
churches of new residents when they arrive? _____ (Yes No)

Do churches make personal visits to your home on a regular basis? _____ (Yes No)

Do you enquire of new residents any past church links or attendances? __ (Yes No)

Are arrangements made for your
residents to attend worship in local churches? _____ (Yes No)

General

Would you like someone to contact you and
explain in more detail the purpose of this survey? _____ (Yes No)

If you have any constructive or critical comments to make on the survey,
please make them on the reverse side of this questionnaire.

Thank you for your time in replying;
we hope to keep in contact once the survey is completed.

An overview of the surveys sent to churches and residential homes

It was found to be important to have a variety of different services in residential homes, although any regular service was better than none, with posters advertising that services will take place. The inclusion of hymns is important, especially those that are well-known. It was stressed in several replies that time for a chat after the service was, in many cases, as important as the service itself.

The value of prayer and study groups depends upon the attention span and general mental alertness of residents.

Better relations between churches and residential homes can be encouraged and recognised by establishing personal contact with members of staff; churches can try to become involved at staff inductions emphasising the spiritual needs of all residents, including those with no stated faith. Links can be established by inviting clergy and lay visitors to homes, and through the use of a 'Newcomer's Card' which can be returned to the church when a new resident arrives at a home. Generally, communication between homes and churches regarding 'new arrivals', illness, hospitalisation or death of residents will foster good working relations.

Churches are able to build up relationships with individual elderly residents by having groups for older people at the church and roles for older people within the church. Transport arrangements can be made to bring people to church for services; the housebound can be visited and tapes of services and other practical help can be given.

Within churches, link-carer systems with approximately one member to ten other (elderly) people can be established. If the link is successful it may be continued should an elderly person move to a residential home. A change of minister can leave elderly people feeling unsettled, so link carers can be used to ensure continuity and provide reassurance during an interregnum. It is important that training is provided for lay visitors to homes, and for those assisting at services and other acts of worship in residential and care homes.

In conclusion: There are many areas where there are needs to be addressed. The committee of Churches Together looking at the Care of Older People suggests that churches concentrate on the establishment of link-carer systems and training for lay people involved in the spiritual care of older people. At the same time they should not lose sight of the importance of communication with the managers and staff running residential homes. Finally, maximum use must be made of the resources available so that the load is spread between the churches in the locality.

To consider

Are the churches in your community doing enough to ensure that the spiritual needs of the elderly are being met adequately? God loves the elderly whether they live in residential homes or in their own homes, and he has a special place in his heart for them. How may you or your church help to make their final years ones marked by peace, joy and dignity?

To do

For more information on how you may conduct a similar survey in your area, or for the results of these questionnaires, write to:

The Chairman
The Subcommittee of
    Churches Together looking at the Care of Older People
Southgate Community Centre
Bury St Edmunds
IP33 2PJ

Chapter 11

GOD'S PARADIGM

Overview: This chapter shows that God wants young and old
to work together to advance Christ's kingdom.

Together is better

Have you ever heard older members of your congregation say, 'I've had a
good innings. Now it's time I stepped aside and left things to the young
folk'? Some people believe they are too old to be of any meaningful
service to their churches. Others selfishly retire at a certain age in order to
live out their days basking in the sun. In the light of the many examples of
the elderly serving God up to the day they died, it is a modern heresy to
think that old age necessarily disqualifies one from serving the Lord.

Of course, it is ludicrous to think that people of 80 can keep up with
people of 30 when it comes to stamina, dexterity and general wellness.
Nevertheless, it is equally ludicrous to imagine that people in their 20s can
hope to have the wisdom of people over twice their age. Yet God calls both
to kingdom work. This is God's paradigm – old and young working in
unison towards the same goal. We see evidence of this model in Joel 2:28:
'And it shall come to pass afterward, that I will pour out my spirit on all
flesh; your sons and your daughters shall prophesy, your old men shall
dream dreams, and your young men shall see visions.'

The Bible contains many examples of this principle in action, but one of
the best examples of this is seen in 2 Chronicles 24. I especially like this
chapter because it proves once and for all that even at a very tender age
we are never barred from serving God: Joash was 7 years old when he
began to reign as king of Israel. The youth was looked after lovingly by the
old priest Jehoiada who clearly had raised him properly, for the chronicler
records: 'And Joash did what was right in the eyes of the Lord' (2
Chronicles 24:2). This is the highest accolade a king of Israel may merit.

Further evidence of how God's paradigm works is seen some sixteen years
later when the king, now aged 23, noticed that the treasury was in short

supply, and the Temple and its services had seriously deteriorated. He began a massive renovation project, combining his energies with the wise counsel of Jehoiada. The end result? The Temple was restored; the treasury was operating in the black; and worship and praise became a hallmark of Jewish services in the restored sanctuary. (2 Chronicles 24:13-14)

Leaders must teach their congregations that all of God's people are to be included in the Church's mission. That said, none of us are vital or wise enough in our own strength to serve God adequately. This means that the best way to serve God is for old and young to work in concert, not independent of each other. Moreover, the ultimate doer of what needs to be done is God, but in his scheme for getting things done in this universe, a key factor is human participation; and old and young together is the best way to go about it. Consider: Samuel anointed David. Naomi counselled Ruth. Paul encouraged Timothy. Clearly, old and young work best in partnership!

David Waite, younger brother of Terry, told me of a contemporary example of this principle. He said that Terry's visits to church at age 4 were at the invitation of an old man who lived nearby. Through the old man, Terry's faith was birthed. That faith later influenced David's path to faith in Christ. Subsequently, when Terry was held hostage in Lebanon, this same faith comforted the Waite family during the silent years before Terry's release. Think what may have happened if the old man hadn't taken Terry to church.

All Saints' Church, Sidmouth, practises the principle of old and young working together. Will Cravens who heads Young Life, an outreach to the youth of east-Devon, says: 'With the help of the people at All Saints and other churches here, my wife Lisa and I work in partnership with the churches of Sidmouth. There aren't masses of converts, but we're encouraged by what we see God doing. Lives are being changed. Kids meet Christ, and as they meet older Christians, relationships are formed.'

Do not despise youth

One old man I know said, 'Youth is wasted on the wrong people!' I disagree. David was a youth when the prophet Samuel anointed him for service to the nation (1 Samuel 16:13). Not long after, Israel was at war with the Philistines, a pugnacious tribe from Canaan. Their destruction of Shiloh, the centre of Hebrew worship, and the capture of the Ark of the Covenant were 'grievous blows to Israel'.[1] To their lasting shame, the elders were too scared to defend Israel against the Philistines' champion, the outsized Goliath. Only young David was bold enough to act in defence of his God and his nation's honour. The account is told in 1 Samuel 17:12-58, but I prefer to imagine it in a modern setting:

David is wearing his prize ruby nose-stud and his low-riding Tommy Hilfiger trousers. He rolls up on his skateboard to the scene of the impasse. He hears Goliath cursing God and says, 'Yo, that Dude can't be dissing the Lord like that. Lemme at 'im!'

Some soldiers try to hold him back, but at 8 stone 2 and 5 feet tall, he easily wriggles free, demanding: 'Lemme at the big Dude!' King Saul is impressed and indicates that he may fight the giant. 'You boy. If you expect to do any good, take my flack jacket, helmet and Uzzi.' The king presses them on the boy. David shakes his head and holds up his slingshot. 'This baby is all I need, Man.'

Meanwhile, Goliath can't believe his eyes. Roaring with laughter, he growls, 'What? You have the backing of your whole army, and you send a boy out to do a man's job? I'll eat this little squirt for breakfast!' Goliath brandishes his AK-47 and his surface-to-air rocket launcher. David, feeling the glory of the Lord come upon him, replies, 'Dude, you come to me with your military gear, but I come to you in the name of the Lord of hosts, the God of the armies of Israel, whom you have defiled. You are about to become history! Take that!' David lets his sling fly, killing the blustering and profane giant. The Philistines are so unnerved by the boy's courage that they flee back into the hills. All of Israel praises the boy warrior.

Elders must never forget that Jesus taught that the Kingdom of God belongs to children (Matthew 18:3; 19:14). By this, he means that the elders do not have a monopoly when it comes to serving God effectively. Still, youth routinely come in for some bad treatment. The Reverend Pat Green, an Assemblies of God missionary, tells the story of 'Charles', an African who became a Christian. God told him to share his new faith with others. In a matter of months, Charles had led fifteen men to Christ. The new Christians wanted to be baptised, so they sent for a missionary from the south of the country. After interviewing each of the converts, he announced he would baptise all but one. 'I am afraid I cannot baptise Charles,' he said gravely, 'because at age 10, I feel Charles is too young to understand the commitment he is making.' The men all protested, telling the missionary that it was Charles who led them to faith. In the end, Charles was baptised.

Elderly Christians must be prepared to accept youngsters. Will Cravens pointed out that the churches in Sidmouth are reaching out in love to him and the youngsters, despite the differences in age and cultures. 'We've received financial gifts from local churches which help us send the kids to camp where they have fun and are taught about what it means to follow Jesus Christ. We know the congregations pray regularly for our outreach and for us. My wife Lisa and I couldn't do our work without the support of the older men and women in Sidmouth's churches.'

In many churches around the country, elderly and young work in harmony in reaching out to the community. Through financial giving, prayer chains, counselling, Meals-on-Wheels, drama, Sunday schools, visitation, beach ministries and rave outreaches, the churches are reaching the whole community, not just one segment.

Evangelist J. John's ministry started through the encouragement of an older, more mature Christian well over twenty years ago. Today, John is hardly an old man, but he has had plenty of experience as one of Britain's foremost evangelists. He longs for revival, but he told me he was worried about one thing: 'We aren't helping younger people to carry the Gospel to our nation. I'm worried that there aren't enough evangelists. The problem is we don't see evangelism as a clear mandate – it isn't high enough on the church's agenda. We're not passing the baton on to the next generation.'

According to J. John, 'We need to go back to basics. The Great Commission says three things: "Go out and make disciples; baptise them – that is marking them; and teach them all that I have commanded you." That is, we must help the disciples mature. Some churches get part of this three-fold command right. But they fall down on other parts. We need to get all three right – making disciples, marking them, and maturing them.'

So does John practise what he preaches? Yes, says David McDougall who ministers in the United Kingdom and the Ukraine. He credits J. John and the Philo Trust, the charity that supports John's ministry, with his start in evangelism. 'J. John has trained and encouraged me so much in my calling as an evangelist. Over the past seven years, I have been in relationship with J. John. He has invited me to join him on several occasions . . . J. John is a good friend and mentor to me.'

God's army

The young and the old have roles to play. Each has strengths and weaknesses. The experience of living many years may lead to a more mature faith (Romans 5:3), and weathering temptations leads to patience and learning more about God's holiness (Luke 8:15). Since this is so, old men and women qualify as the generals who offer their acquired wisdom to the younger, less experienced soldiers, who in turn have the energy, strength and pluck to serve God dynamically (Genesis 49:8-9; Deuteronomy 33:22).

Satan knows a unified Church is more than his match. His scheme is to use everything at his disposal to set one generation against the other. As long as the Church is divided then its mission on earth is undermined.

Truly, together is better.

Reference

1   Joan Comay and Ronald Brownrigg, *'Philistines' Who's Who in the Bible*, New York: Bonanza Books, 1980, p. 315.

Epilogue

THE PATH TAKEN –
A MISSIONARY'S MEMOIR

Our teacher stood before us. His faded black cassock hung from thin shoulder blades like worn-out curtains. Wispy ashen cables crosshatched his creased forehead; dense blue cordage bristled on the back of his mottled hand as he clutched a stub of chalk.

'Ahem.'

Like grazing cattle staring at a passing car, the class looked up.

Only the day before, I found his photograph in a yearbook. A head-and-shoulder profile, all the rage during the Jazz Age. He had been named head boy for the year 1928. His hair was glossy in those days: a pomaded, peaked, pompadour. His eyes were lucid; curious, direct – not shielded beneath sore red lids and a thatched brow. The Great Depression, the War, and generations of lusty schoolboys lay ahead.

David Hamilton dug his elbow into John Barns.

'Sir, what made you become a – a teacher?'

David wanted to say *priest*, but he said *teacher*. My friends rolled their eyes at the question. But I watched the teacher as a blackbird watches a gardener turning friable black soil with a spade.

The teacher glanced at each boy's face until he saw mine. I thought the light in his eyes smouldered, like the cherry red coals of a fire banked early on a winter's day and then forgotten. I looked at my hands.

'Well, Sir?' prompted Hamilton.

'Open your books on page 51, please,' was all the teacher said.

The boys groaned. Gradually, the chatter and page turning ceased. Silence descended as we read 'The Road Not Taken' a poem by Robert Frost. The only sound was the tick-ticking of the clock below the crucifix. My eyes skimmed the clean line of words until I reached the last stanza:

Two roads diverged in a wood, and I –
I took the one less travelled by,
and that has made all the difference.

I thought of the young man in that picture in the yearbook. He might have chosen any road – why the road of a priest? When the bell had gone, I remained behind.

'Sir?'

My teacher arched his eyebrows.

'What was the other road – I mean the road you didn't choose?'

He smiled. 'Oh, there never was another road. It only seemed to be there.'

'Thank you, Sir,' I said stiffly. I picked up my book and left the room.

'Christ Almighty, where've you been?'

It was David Hamilton. I started toward him. Suddenly, I stopped and walked the other way.

'Oi! Where're you going?'

Without looking back, I called over my shoulder: 'Somewhere different.'

Helpful Addresses

Information provided courtesy of Help the Aged

Your **Health Authority** produces lists of health practitioners (opticians, dentists, doctors, etc.) in your area. If you can't find a doctor who will accept you into their practice, then it is the Health Authority's responsibility to find one for you.

Your **Community Health Council** (Local Health Council if you are in Scotland) can give you information on local health services. They can also offer advice if you are having problems with your doctor, or with any other health services. They should be in the phone book under 'C'.

The **Patients' Association** can offer advice and information on health issues such as patients' rights, complaints procedures and appropriate self-help groups:

PO Box 935
Harrow
HA1 3YJ

Tel: 020 8423 8999 (Helpline)

CancerBACUP and **CancerLink** provide information and support services to people with cancer and their families:

CancerBACUP
3 Bath Place
Rivington Street
London
EC2A 3JR

Tel: 0808 800 1234 (Freephone helpline)

CancerLink
11-21 Northdown Street
London
N1 9BN

Tel: 0800 132 905 (Information line)

Macmillan Cancer Relief and **Marie Curie Cancer Care** provide specialist nurses to assist in caring for people with cancer:

Macmillan Cancer Relief
Anchor House
15-19 Britten Street
London
SW3 3TZ

Tel: 020 7351 7811

Marie Curie Cancer Care
28 Belgrave Square
London
SW1X 8QG

Tel: 020 7235 3325

The **British Heart Foundation** and the **British Lung Foundation** can offer advice to people suffering from heart and lung problems:

British Heart Foundation
14 Fitzhardinge Street
London
W1H 4DH

Tel: 020 7935 0185

British Lung Foundation
78 Hatton Garden
London
EC1N 8LD

Tel: 020 7831 5831

The **RNIB** and the **RNID** can offer expert advice and information to people with visual impairment or hearing problems.

RNIB (Royal National Institute for the Blind)
224 Great Portland Street
London
W1N 6AA

Tel: 020 7388 1266
     0345 66 99 99 (Helpline)

RNID (Royal National Institute for the Deaf)
19-23 Featherstone Street
London
EC1Y 8SL

Tel: 020-7296 8000

Similarly, many of the voluntary organisations listed in Chapter 9, such as the Alzheimer's Society, can offer specialist advice and support on particular medical conditions.

The **Medical Advisory Service** offers information on medical conditions and treatments on 020 8994 9874 (Mon-Fri: 6-9pm). All information is given by a trained nurse.

The **Health Information Line** is a freephone line, which provides confidential information on common diseases and conditions, and on NHS services. Call 0800 66 55 44 (Mon-Fri: 10am-5pm).

Help the Aged produce free advice leaflets and information sheets on health issues including:

- Better Hearing
- Incontinence
- Better Sight
- Keeping Mobile
- Fitter Feet, Managing Your Medicines, Healthy Eating – Information Sheet No 7
- Getting an Operation, Information Sheet No 14
- Going into Hospital, Information Sheet No 9
- Health Benefits (explains who is entitled to free or reduced cost prescriptions, sight tests, glasses, etc.) Information Sheet No 22
- Coming out of Hospital, Age Concern – Fact Sheet No 5
- Dental Care in Retirement.

The above can be obtained by calling 0800 00 99 66.

Other relevant addresses

Carers' National Association
20-25 Glasshouse Yard
London
EC1A 4JS

Tel: 020 7490 8818

Carers' line: 0808 808 7777

Counsel and Care
Twyman House
16 Bonny Street
London
NW1 9PG

Helpline: 0845 300 7585 (10:30am-4pm)

Disablement Income Group
PO Box 5743
Finchingfield
Essex
CM7 4PW

Tel: 01371 811 621

Hospice Information Service
St Christopher's Hospice
51-59 Lawrie Park Road
London
SE26 6DZ

Tel: 020 8778 9252

Local Government Ombudsman Commission for Local Administration
21 Queen Anne's Gate
London
SW1H 9BU

The United Kingdom Home Care Association
42 Banstead Road
Carshalton
Surrey
SM5 3NW

Tel: 020 8288 1557 13

Legislation and Case Law

Most people requiring community care will not need to be familiar with legislation and case law. However, if problems should arise and you need to make a complaint it can put you in a stronger position if you are able to quote the relevant law. Listed here are the main sources of law in this area.

For further advice contact Help the Aged's free advice line SeniorLine on 0808 800 6565.

NHS & Community Care Act 1990: s. 47(1) and (2) obliges the local authority to carry out an assessment of need for anybody in their area who it appears to them may need their services.

Chronically Sick & Disabled Person's Act 1970: s. 2 details the services that a local authority might provide. Carer's (Recognition and Services) Act 1995, entitles a carer to a separate assessment of need from social services.

R v Gloucester County Council ex parte Barry – House of Lords 1997: This case established that it is perfectly legitimate for a local authority to take its own resources into account when setting its eligibility criteria for services. Once a person has been assessed as having particular needs, however, the local authority is then obliged to provide the services.

Part III of the National Assistance Act 1948 covers the local authority's responsibilities to provide residential accommodation. This includes paying for somebody to be placed in a private residential home.

Health & Social Services & Social Security Adjudication Act (HASSASSA) 1983: s. 17(3) gives the local authority the power to make a 'reasonable charge' for domiciliary care services.

R v Lancashire County Council ex parte Ingham – Court of Appeal – 1996: Allowed local authorities to choose the cheapest option when deciding which services to provide.

Community Care (Direct Payments) Act 1996, gives local authorities the power to make direct payments in place of services.

For further information, please contact:

Information Department
Help the Aged
St James' Walk
London
EC1R OBE

SeniorLine is the free welfare rights advice and information service run by Help the Aged for older people and their carers. Trained advice workers offer free, confidential and impartial advice about:

- Welfare and disability benefits

- Community and residential care

- Housing options and adaptations

- Access to health and community services

- Equipment to assist independence

- Support for carers

- Agencies offering local practical help.

Telephone: 0808 800 6565

Textphone (Minicom): 0800 26 96 26 (9am to 4pm, Monday to Friday).

Your call will be free of charge.

Help the Aged is a registered charity No. 272786, registered in England.

ACKNOWLEDGEMENTS

The publishers wish to express their gratitude to the following for permission to include copyright material in this book:

Augsburg Fortress Press, Box 1209, Minneapolis, MN 55440-1209, for the extracts from the *Revised Standard Version of the Bible* © 1946, 1952, and 1971 by the Division of Christian Education of the National Council of the Churches of Christ in the USA. All rights reserved.

The *Guardian*, 119 Farringdon Road, London, EC1R 3ER, for the extracts from *Guardian Unlimited* Online.

David Higham Associates Ltd, 5/8 Lower John Street, Golden Square, London, W1R 4HA, for the extract from *Christ and the Media* by Malcolm Muggeridge, published by Eerdmans, Grand Rapids, USA, 1978.

Kingsway Publications, Lottbridge Drove, Eastbourne, BN23 6NT for the extract from *Classics from Watchman Nee*, volume 2, © Angus I. Kinnear, published by Kingsway Publications.

NIH Neurological Institute, PO Box 5801, Bethesda, MD 20824, USA, for the facts about stroke taken from their website.

Random House Inc, 201 East 50th Street, New York, NY 10022, USA, for the extract from *Future Shock* by Alvin Toffler (p. 257), Random House NY, 1970.

The Scout Association of Australia, PO Box 325, Five Docks, NSW 2046, Australia, for the quotation from *Youth Suicide Prevention Parents' Guidebook*.

The Society for the Protection of Unborn Children, Phyllis Bowman House, 5/6 St Matthew Street, Westminster, London, SW1P 2JT, for the extract from *Euthanasia by Deception*, SPUC News Release, October 1999.

The Voluntary Euthanasia Society, 13 Prince of Wales Terrace, London, W8 5PG, UK, for extracts from their website: http://www.ves.org.uk